WITHDRAWN

The Merrill Studies
in
Light in August

Compiled by

M. Thomas Inge
Virginia Commonwealth University

Charles E. Merrill Publishing Company
A Bell & Howell Company
Columbus, Ohio

For Scott Thomas Inge

CHARLES E. MERRILL STUDIES

Under the General Editorship of
Matthew J. Bruccoli and Joseph Katz

Copyright © 1971 by Charles E. Merrill Publishing Company, Columbus, Ohio. All rights reserved. No part of this book may be reproduced in any form, electronic or mechanical, including photocopy, recording, or any information storage and retrieval system without the permission in writing from the publisher.

ISBN: 0–675–09219–1

Library of Congress Catalog Number: 73–148520

1 2 3 4 5 6 7 8 9—79 78 77 76 75 74 73 72 71

Printed in the United States of America

Preface

William Faulkner's seventh published novel, *Light in August,* has increased steadily in popularity and reputation since its appearance in 1932. It is considered by many an excellent place to begin reading Faulkner, because it is traditional enough in style and structure not to discourage the reader unused to Faulkner's more radical techniques, yet innovative enough to display the hand of a truly advanced master at work in the art of fiction. While it is a part of the larger scheme of a chronicle of the fictional Yoknapatawpha County and contains characters who reappear in other works, it is also a novel quite independent of the others and does not require prior familiarity with the *dramatis personae* for full comprehension. In addition, the central concern of the novel—the irrational reactions of man to the categories of race and color —is one whose significance has grown to threatening proportions over the last two decades. Yet it does not partake of propaganda or polemic in that Faulkner uses racial identity as a metaphor for writing about man's universal search for identity and self-understanding in an increasingly disoriented world. Some critics have grown to consider *Light in August* the author's masterwork, with much justification.

Full critical appreciation of the novel in terms of theme and artistry has not come easily or quickly. The first reviewers were somewhat unsettled by the seemingly disjointed plot structure which combined the disparate stories of Joe Christmas and Lena Grove, by the blatant treatment of social attitudes in the South regarding miscegenation, and by the depiction of the sordid details and raw violence of prostitution, nymphomania, decapitation, and castration. The *Bookman* included the novel in its list of books recommended for Christmas giving under the category of "Intellectual Blood and Thunder." Yet a large proportion of the reviews were favorable because the critics appear to have realized, albeit with some uncertainty, that something more significant was going on here than the production of another chapter in the decline of the South, something they had come to expect of the author of *Sanctuary* and "A Rose for Emily," both issued in books the year before.

Within a few years of its publication, *Light in August* had become the subject of technical and critical explication, although several errors in reading the novel were early perpetrated and consistently repeated for the following three decades. The two most frequent misreadings were that Joe Christmas was definitely of mixed blood and that Gail Hightower died at the conclusion of the novel. Indeed, even the most careful and astute critics committed the latter error, but it is only fair to point out that the text is slightly ambiguous on the point. Faulkner corrected the error in his discussions at the University of Virginia, where he refuted as well the theory that the title of the book was drawn from a Southern phrase, that a mare or a cow is "light in August" after delivery of her young. (For an enumeration of some sixteen other errors, the reader may consult Floyd C. Watkins, "Faulkner and His Critics," *Texas Studies in Literature and Language,* x (Summer 1968), 317–329.

As Faulkner criticism matured during the fifties and sixties, critics resolved the technical complexities of the novel and began to explore its roots in the literary traditions and culture of Western civilization—its use of pagan myth and ritual, its parallels with the Passion story of Jesus Christ, and its revival of the classical archetype of the tragic hero for use in a contemporary fictional tragedy. Proceeding in these various directions, much of the criticism has been, interestingly enough, complementary rather than contradictory. Step by step, they have revealed for our appreciation the aesthetic virtues of a highly accomplished work of art, the depths of which have yet fully to be sounded.

In making selections for this volume, I have evaluated over 170 essays, reviews or parts of books devoted to *Light in August*. Although at least three-quarters of this criticism makes little contribution to an understanding of the novel, the remainder is rich and diverse enough to make the final selection difficult. Space limitations and permission problems have necessitated the exclusion of several essays I would have preferred to include, yet the pieces represented make, I believe, substantial contributions to Faulkner criticism. My preference has been for whole essays reprinted without abridgement and which stand independent of book-length critical studies readily available in their original form. Of the fourteen selections, ten are reprinted here for the first time in an anthology of criticism. All together, they make a considerable argument for considering *Light in August* one of Faulkner's best achievements in the craft of fiction.

Contents

1. Backgrounds and Sources

2. Contemporary Reviews

3. Critical Essays

1. Backgrounds and Sources

Comments on *Light in August*

Q. Sir, in another one of your stories, "Percy Grimm," do you think that the type of person that is exemplified there is prevalent in the South today, perhaps in the White Citizens Councils?

A. I wouldn't say prevalent, he exists everywhere, I wrote that book in 1932 before I'd ever heard of Hitler's Storm Troopers, what he was was a Nazi Storm Trooper, but then I'd never heard of one then, and he's not prevalent but he's everywhere. I wouldn't say that there are more of him in the South, but I would say that there are probably more of him in the White Citizens Council than anywhere else in the South, but I think you find him everywhere, in all countries, in all people.

Q. Sir, was Percy Grimm ever punished for his crime?

A. I think in time that every Storm Trooper suffers for it. He don't suffer any retribution, any stroke of lightning from the gods, but he's got to live with himself, and there comes a time when you've got to live with that, when you're too old and the fire which enables you to get a certain amount of hysterical adrenalic pleasure out of things like that is gone, and all you have left is to remember what you did and you probably wonder why in God's name you did things like that, and you have to live with it, and I think that quite often unexplained suicides go back to some man who has done something like that and he gets old, and he's got to live with it, and decides it's not worth living with it.

Q. This is a question about *Light in August*. Could you tell me your purpose in placing the chapter about Hightower's early life in the end of the novel, that is, rather than when Hightower first appears?

A. It may be this. Unless a book follows a simple direct line such as a story of adventure, it becomes a series of pieces. It's a good deal like dressing a showcase window. It takes a certain amount of judgment and taste to arrange the different pieces in the most

From *Faulkner in the University*, ed. by Frederick L. Gwynne and Joseph L. Blotner (Charlottesville: The University Press of Virginia, 1959). Excerpts taken from pp. 41–199. Reprinted by permission of The University Press of Virginia.

effective place in juxtaposition to one another. That was the reason. It seemed to me that was the most effective place to put that, to underline the tragedy of Christmas's story by the tragedy of his antithesis, a man who—Hightower was a man who wanted to be better than he was afraid he would. He had failed his wife. Here was another chance he had, and he failed his Christian oath as a man of God, and he escaped into his past where some member of his family was brave enough to match the moment. But it was put at that point in the book, I think, because I thought that was the most effective place for it.

Q. Sir, in *Light in August* the central character Joe Christmas had most of his troubles and persecutions and in his search to find himself was based on his belief that he was part Negro and yet it's never made really clear that he is. Was he supposed to be part Negro, or was this supposed to add to the tragic irony of the story?

A. I think that was his tragedy—he didn't know what he was, and so he was nothing. He deliberately evicted himself from the human race because he didn't know which he was. That was his tragedy, that to me was the tragic, central idea of the story—that he didn't know what he was, and there was no way possible in life for him to find out. Which to me is the most tragic condition a man could find himself in—not to know what he is and to know that he will never know.

Q. Sir, if he is not—does not definitely have Negro blood, well, what is the significance of Gavin Stevens's surmise there at the end when he explains that there's a conflict of blood? That is only a guess that stands for a guess and not a final knowledge of—?

A. Yes, that is an assumption, a rationalization which Stevens made. That is, the people that destroyed him made rationalizations about what he was. They decided what he was. But Christmas himself didn't know and he evicted himself from mankind.

.   .   .   .

Q. Mr. Faulkner, in working out the situation of Joe Christmas, did you deliberately have in mind a correspondence between his situation and Oedipus, for example, as has recently been brought out in an essay published in the *Virginia Quarterly* magazine?

A. No, not deliberately and not consciously. That's another matter of the writer reaching back into the lumber room of his memory for whatever he needs to create the character or the situation, and the similarity is there but it was not by deliberate intent. It was by coincidence—not accident but by coincidence.

Q. Sir, in *Light in August* much of the action comes back to the theme or the picture of a column of yellow smoke coming up from Joanna Burden's cabin. I was wondering—you had said that in *The Sound and the Fury* you got the idea of the story from seeing a little girl like Caddy in a tree. I was wondering whether that happened with *Light in August*. Perhaps that was a theme that you had seen and that you started from in that story.

A. No, that story began with Lena Grove, the idea of the young girl with nothing, pregnant, determined to find her sweetheart. It was—that was out of my admiration for women, for the courage and endurance of women. As I told that story I had to get more and more into it, but that was mainly the story of Lena Grove.

. . . .

Q. In *Light in August* do you feel that Rev. Hightower dies feeling that he has achieved a certain kind of salvation—some sort of salvation?

A. He didn't die. He had wrecked his life. He had failed his wife. He had failed himself, but there was one thing that he still had—which was the brave grandfather that galloped into the town to burn the Yankee stores, and at least he had that. Everything else was gone, but since he had been a man of God he still tried to be a man of God and he could not destroy himself. But he had destroyed himself but he still couldn't take his own life. He had to endure, to live, but that was one thing that was pure and fine that he had—was the memory of his grandfather, who had been brave.

. . . .

Q. Sir, you indicated before that *A Fable* was a departure in that—insofar that it was the only book that was written from an absolute idea with regular city limits to it. But I find—at least, *I* find—that the basic crucifixion image in *A Fable* occurs over and over again in your books. It occurs in *Light in August*. It happens in a kind of way even in *Sanctuary*. It happens in *Requiem for a Nun* especially, with Nancy. Isn't *A Fable* simply a more positive way of approaching the problem?

A. As a result, it might be. Remember, the writer must write out of his background. He must write out of what he knows and the Christian legend is part of any Christian's background, especially the background of a country boy, a Southern country boy. My life was passed, my childhood, in a very small Mississippi town, and that was a part of my background. I grew up with that. I assimilated that, took that in without even knowing it. It's just there. It has nothing to do with how much of it I might believe or disbelieve—it's just there.

. . . Q. Mr. Faulkner, is your opinion of Tennyson in *Light in August*, as expressed by Hightower's remark that reading Tennyson is "like listening in a cathedral to a eunuch chanting in a language he does not even need to not understand," is that your opinion of Tennyson?

A. No sir, that was Hightower's opinion, and I'm not responsible for his opinion. I have a different opinion of Tennyson myself, that when I was younger, I read Tennyson with a great deal of pleasure. I can't read him at all now.

Q. Referring to an earlier question, did you say that *Light in August* argues . . . for the acceptance of an inevitably tragic view of life?

A. I wouldn't think so. That the only person in that book that accepted a tragic view of life was Christmas because he didn't know what he was and so he deliberately repudiated man. He didn't belong to man any longer, he deliberately repudiated man. The others seemed to me to have had a very fine belief in life, in the basic possibility for happiness and goodness—Byron Bunch and Lena Grove, to have gone to all that trouble.

Q. Mr. Faulkner, did you intend any Christ symbolism in *Light in August* in Joe Christmas?

A. No, that's a matter of reaching into the lumber room to get out something which seems to the writer the most effective way to tell what he is trying to tell. And that comes back to the notion that there are so few plots to use that sooner or later any writer is going to use something that has been used. And that Christ story is one of the best stories that man has invented, assuming that he did invent that story, and of course it will recur. Everyone that has had the story of Christ and the Passion as a part of his Christian background will in time draw from that. There was no deliberate intent to repeat it. That the people to me come first. The symbolism comes second.

Q. Well, I was just wondering why [for] such a sort of bad man as Joe Christmas you would use Christ, whether. . . .

A. Well, Joe Christmas—I think that you really can't say that any man is good or bad. I grant you there are some exceptions, but man is the victim of himself, or his fellows, or his own nature, or his environment, but no man is good or bad either. He tries to do the best he can within his rights. Now with Christmas, for instance, he didn't know what he was. He knew that he would never know what he was, and his only salvation in order to live with himself was to repudiate mankind, to live outside the human race. And he tried to do that but nobody would let him, the human race itself wouldn't let him. And I don't think he was bad, I think he was tragic. And his tragedy was that he didn't know what he was and would never know, and that to me is the most tragic condition that an individual can have—to not know who he was.

Q. You spoke of titles before, Mr. Faulkner. I'd like to ask you about the origin of *Light in August*.

A. Oh that was—in August in Mississippi there's a few days somewhere about the middle of the month when suddenly there's a foretaste of fall, it's cool, there's a lambence, a luminous quality to the light, as though it came not from just today but from back in the old classic times. It might have fauns and satyrs and the gods and—from Greece, from Olympus in it somewhere. It lasts just for a day or two, then it's gone, but every year in August that occurs in my country, and that's all that title meant, it was just to me a pleasant evocative title because it reminded me of that time, of a luminosity older than our Christian civilization. Maybe the connection was with Lena Grove, who had something of that pagan quality of being able to assume everything, that's—the desire for that child, she was never ashamed of that child whether it had any father or not, she was simply going to follow the conventional laws of the time in which she was and find its father. But as far as she was concerned, she didn't especially need any father for it, any more than the women that—on whom Jupiter begot children were anxious for a home and a father. It was enough to have had the child. And that was all that meant, just that luminous lambent quality of an older light than ours.

John B. Cullen
Floyd C. Watkins

Joe Christmas
and Nelse Patton

At noon one day late in August, when I was a boy fourteen or fifteen, my father Linburn Cullen, who was then a deputy sheriff, was called by telephone and told that a Negro had just killed a woman out north of Oxford and that he should come to join a posse at once. Before leaving, my father instructed me and my older brother to stay at home and keep out of trouble. But as soon as he had gone, we picked up our shotguns and headed to the place where we thought the killer would travel as he fled to the nearest big thicket from the location of his crime.

As we drew near this place, we heard gunfire and saw a big Negro run across the railroad at Saddler's Crossing about two hundred yards ahead of us. At that time I could run like a foxhound and I never lost sight of him until he jumped into a vine-covered ditch leading into Toby Tubby Bottom. He was running along a valley between two hills, and my brother ran down one of them and I the other. In the valley there was one clear place which the criminal would have to cross before he reached the big thicket in Toby Tubby Bottom. I kept my eyes on this opening, and when I reached it, I knew that he was hiding somewhere back up the valley. The posse was coming on, so I knew that soon we would have him. When the Negro, Nelse Patton, saw that I knew he was hiding in the thicket, he attempted to come by me. I yelled for him to halt and when he kept on running, I shot at him with squirrel shot from both barrels of my shotgun. This stopped him. But that was about the first time I had ever shot anything bigger than a cottontail rabbit, and my squirrel shot were far too small to do much damage at that distance.

I reloaded and ran up close to him and told him to put up his hands. He said to my brother, "Mr. Jenks, you knows I'se a good nigger."

From *Old Times in the Faulkner Country*. (Chapel Hill: The University of North Carolina Press, 1961), pp. 89–98. Reprinted by permission of The University of North Carolina Press.

7

"I know you're a good nigger," my brother said, "but get your hands up." But Nelse never did put his hands up.

He was still standing up, and I believe he was trying to get a chance to grab my gun. If he had tried this, I was ready to shoot him between the eyes. Mr. Curt Hartsfield, the sheriff, and his deputy, Mr. Guy Taylor, rode up. When Mr. Taylor searched him, he found in his pocket a bloody razor with one corner broken off. I probably would have been killed if my father had not accidentally shot a big forty-five Colt out of Nelse's hand with a long-distance rifle shot as he went over a high hill north of Oxford.

After turning Nelse over to the sheriff, I went to the scene of the crime. Mrs. Mattie McMillan was lying in the dusty road about seventy-five yards from her home. How she had run that far I do not know. Her head had been severed from her body, all but the neck bone. Dr. Young, who was examining her, found sticking in her neck bone a piece of steel which fitted the gap missing from Nelse's razor.

The news spread over the county like wildfire, and that night at least two thousand people gathered around the jail. Judge Roan came out on the porch and made a plea to the crowd that they let the law take its course. Then Senator W. V. Sullivan made a fiery speech, telling the mob that they would be weaklings and cowards to let such a vicious beast live until morning. Mr. Hartsfield, the sheriff, had left town with the keys to the jail, because he knew people would take them away from him. My father was deputized to guard the jail. Had he had the slightest doubt of Nelse's guilt, he would have talked to the mob. If this had not proved successful, they would have entered the jail over his dead body. After Senator Sullivan's speech, the mob began pitching us boys through the jail windows, and no guard in that jail would have dared shoot one of us. Soon a mob was inside. My brother and I held my father, and the sons of the other guards held theirs. They weren't hard to hold anyway. In this way we took over the lower floor of the jail.

From eight o'clock that night until two in the morning the mob worked to cut through the jail walls into the cells with sledge hammers and crowbars. In the walls were one-by-eight boards placed on top of one another and bolted together. The walls were brick on the outside and steel-lined on the inside. When the mob finally got through and broke the lock off the murderer's cell, Nelse had armed himself with a heavy iron coal-shovel handle.

From a corner near the door, he fought like a tiger, seriously wounding three men. He was then shot to death and thrown out of the jail. Someone (I don't know who) cut his ears off, scalped him, cut his testicles out, tied a rope around his neck, tied him to a car, and dragged his body around the streets. Then they hanged him to a walnut-tree limb just outside the south entrance to the courthouse. They had torn his clothes off dragging him around, and my father bought a new pair of overalls and put them on him before the next morning.

Nelse Patton's crime and the lynching of Nelse are more widely known than anything else of this kind that ever happened in Lafayette County. William Faulkner was eleven years old at the time, and since he has spent most of his life in this community, he must have heard numerous stories about the Patton case. Faulkner has written about many lynchings in his books, and I believe that several of them are generally based on the story of Nelse Patton.

In some ways, the entire book of *Light in August* is centered around the lynching of Joe Christmas, and it seems to me that Faulkner used the stories he had heard about the Nelse Patton case. There are a number of parallels between the stories of Nelse and Joe. Joanna Burden and Mrs. McMillan both lived outside of town, and each of them had her throat cut from ear to ear by a Negro man using a razor. Nelse and Joe both attempted to escape in a similar way over similar terrain. Both of the Negro men were lynched: Nelse was shot in the jail, and Joe was shot in the kitchen of the Reverend Hightower. Senator Sullivan, who incited the mob to riot in Oxford, reminds me a little of Percy Grimm, who led the lynchers in *Light in August*. Both bodies were mutilated, though in slightly different ways. These likenesses seem more important because Faulkner knew more about Nelse Patton's lynching than about any other single episode of that kind.

In *Sanctuary*, also, Faulkner describes almost exactly Nelse Patton's murder of Mrs. McMillan: "... there was a negro murderer in the jail, who had killed his wife; slashed her throat with a razor so that, her whole head tossing further and further backward from the bloody regurgitation of her bubbling throat, she ran out the cabin door and for six or seven steps up the quiet moonlit lane."

Southern newspapers of that period published full-length stories about the lynching of Nelse Patton. *The Lafayette County Press,*

of September 9, 1908, printed the most complete and accurate
account. This story, reprinted below, shows how Southern report-
ers wrote about such crimes in those old days. This is a colorful
(perhaps too much so) and factual version of a story that was of
great interest to William Faulkner. The mistakes are in the original.

NEGRO BRUTE CUTS WOMAN'S THROAT

Mrs. Mattie McMullen, A White Woman The Victim—
Lived But Ten Minutes After The Tragedy. Sheriff
Hartsfield And Posse of Citizens Give Chase and Land
Negro in Jail

Mob Storms Jail and Kills Desperado

Officers and Guards Overpowered, and Failing to Find the
Keys the Orderly Mob Quietly and Deliberately Took Mat-
ters in Their Own Hands, Forced Entrance to Cell Where
Negro Was Confined Negro Armed with Poker Puts Up
Desperate Fight and is Killed.

One of the coldest blooded murders and most brutal crimes
known to the criminal calendar was perputrated one mile north
of town yesterday morning about ten o'clock, when a black brute
of unsavory reputation by the name of Nelse Patton attacked
Mrs. Mattie McMullen,[1] a respected white woman, with a razor,
cutting her throat from ear to ear and causing almost instant
death. Reports as to the cause of the tragedy vary, but as near
as can be learned the partic- are these:

Mrs. McMullen, whose husband was confined at the time in the
county jail at this place, was a hard working woman living alone
with her 17-year-old daughter and two other very small children.
It seems that Mr. McMullen wanted to communicate with his

---

[1] The name was spelled in various ways by the newspapers of the time, and
it is also pronounced several ways. As nearly as I can determine, it is
McMillan.

wife, and as was his custom as such occasions, he called the murderer, who was a "trusty" prisoner at the jail, to carry the missive. Arriving at the house, the negro, who was in an intoxicated condition, walked into the house without knocking and took a seat. Seeing the woman apparently alone and without protection, his animal passion was aroused and he made insulting remarks to her. He was ordered from the house and some angry words passed between them, when the woman started toward the bureau drawer to get her pistol, The brute seeing her design made a rush at the woman from behind and drawing the razor cut her throat from ear to ear, almost severing the head from the body. The dying woman rushed out of the house, and the daughter hearing the confusion rushed in, and was instantly grabbed by the negro. Jerking herself from the brutes grasp, she followed her mother who had fallen dead a few yards from the house. The daughter's screams alarmed the neighbors who quickly responded to call and immediately sent in a hurried telephone message to the Press office to summons officers and a physician, who in less than twenty minutes were on the way to the scene of the murder. The news spread like wild fire and it was but a short while until the sheriff was joined by a posse of citizens all in hot and close pursuit of the brute. After chasing the negro three or four miles over fences, through briars and fields he suddenly ran amuck of Johnny Cullen, the 14-year-old son of Lin Cullen, who was out with a double-barreled shotgun. Seeing the negro coming towards him, he called a halt, but the negro paid no attention to the command and the boy let him have a load of No. 5 shot in the chest, which slackened his speed but did not stop him. The boy gave him another charge in the left arm and side which stopped him. The negro was at once surrounded by his pursuers and gladly gave up. Over a hundred shots were fired from all kinds of weapons but the negro was out of range. Being weak from loss of blood, the brute was put on a horse and hurried to jail.

As soon as the news spread of the capture, hundreds of people began to gather around the jail and in small groups about the street. They were not indulging in idle threats, but from the seriousness of their expression one could see the negro's fate was sealed.

Between nine and ten o'clock the crowd began swelling to large proportions about the jail. Speeches were made advocating letting the law take its course and vice-versa, but patience had fallen far

short of being a virtue in a crowd like that. One wild shout went
up, with a rush the crowd advanced on the jail, pushing open doors
and jumping through windows. Officers and guards were overpowered and disarmed. The keys could not be found, but the
hardware stores and blacksmith shops were made to furnish the
necessary tools and a set of quiet and determined men plied them.
Four and one-half hours of hard and persistent work it took to
break through the thick walls of steel and masonry. The hall was
at last reached, and a search of the cell occupied by that black
fiend incarnate was made. It was at last found and broken into.
Crouched and cringing in a dark corner of the cell, with the gleam
of murder in his eye stood the miserable wretch armed with an
iron poker awaiting the advance. In one, two, thee order the mob
entered the cell, and in the same order the iron decended upon
their heads, blood flew, the negro having all the advantage in his
dark corner, held the crowd at bay and refused to come out. Only
one thing was left to do. It was done. 26 pistol shots vibrated
throughout the corridors of the solid old jail, and when the smoke
cleared away the limp and lifeless body of the brute told the story.

The body was hustled down stairs to terra-firma, the rope was
produced, the hangmans noose properly adjusted about the neck,
and the drag to the court house yard began.

This morning the passerby saw the lifeless body of a negro
suspended from a tree—it told the tale, that the murder of a
white woman had been avenged—the public had done their duty.
Following is the verdict of the Corners Jury:

We the Coroners Jury of inquest impaneled and sworn to
investigate the death of Nelse Patton, colored find after inspecting
the body and examining necessary witnesses that to the best of
our knowledge and belief, the said Nelse Patton came to his death
from gunshot or pistol wounds inflicted by parties to us unknown.
That any one of a number of wounds would have been sufficient
to cause death. We find further that Sheriff J. C. Hartsfield and
his deputies were dilllgent in their efforts to protect said Nelse
Patton from the time of his arrest until they were overpowered
by a mob of several hundred men who stormed the jail and dug
their way through the walls until they reached the cell in which
said Nelse Patton was confined and that said officers never sur-
rendered the keys of jail or cells but that the locks were forced
by some party or parties to us unknown and that the said Nelse
Patton was shot with pistols or guns while in his cell and while
attempting to protect himself with an iron rod. We further find

that the said Nelse Patton was dead berore being brought from the jail and being hung.

Respectfully submitted,
E. O. Davidson
R. S. Adams
P. E. Matthews
B. P. Gray
A. F. Calloway
F. Wood

The papers gave special attention to Senator Sullivan's role in the lynching. This is a quotation from the Jackson *Daily Clarion-Ledger*, of Thursday morning, September 10, 1908. Errors are again reproduced from the original.

SULLIVAN'S HOT TALK ON OXFORD LYNCHING

FORMER UNITED STATES SENATOR FROM MISSISSIPPI LED THE MOB

(Associated Press Report)

Memphis, Tenn., Sept. 9.—A special from Oxford, Miss., quotes former U.S. Senator W. V. Sullivan as follows, with reference to the lynching of last night:

"I led the mob which lynched Nelse Patton and I am proud of it.

"I directed every movement of the mob, and I did everything I could to see that he was lynched.

"Cut a white woman's throat? and a negro? Of course I wanted him lynched.

"I saw his body dangling from a tree this morning and I am glad of it.

"When I heard of the horrible crime, I started to work immediately to get a mob. I did all I could to raise one. I was at the jail last night and I heard Judge Roane advise against lynching. I got up immediately after and urged the mob to lynch Patton.

"I aroused the mob and directed them to storm the jail.

"I had my revolver, but did not use it. I gave it to a deputy sheriff and told him: 'Shoot Patton and shoot to kill.'

"He used the revolver and shot. I suppose the bullets from my gun were some of those that killed the negro.

"I don't care what investigation is made, or what are the consequences. I am willing to stand them.

"I wouldn't mind standing the consequences any time for lynching a man who cut a white woman's throat. I will lead a mob in such a case any time."

2. Contemporary Reviews

Henry Seidel Canby

The Grain of Life

Those interested in the career of William Faulkner, and they are many, have waited with some concern for the appearance of his next book. They have felt that his earlier stories had shown a powerful grasp upon character and scene, a poetic vision that set him apart from the prosaic realists of the day, but a hurt mind tending with an alarming descent toward morbidity and the macabre. Was he to be another Southerner racked to pieces by his own talents, or a power in American literature?

"Light in August" may not be the final answer, but it is an answer. It is a novel of extraordinary force and insight, incredibly rich in character studies, intensely vivid, rising sometimes to poetry, and filled with that spirit of compassion which saves those who look at life too closely from hardness and despair. If the writing is sometimes as slovenly as at other times it is pointed and brilliant, if there are scenes too macabre, characters in whom fantasy transcends its just limits, and an obscurity, or rather, a turgidity in symbolism which is often annoying, this is merely to say that it is not a perfect work of art. Men of Faulkner's experience and training seldom make of their work one perfect chrysoprase; but there is no reason to suppose with this writer that he will be congenitally unable to shape his imagination into its own best form. He needs self-discipline, and the discipline of study and reading, but he can be trusted to find his own way.

The more so, since Faulkner possesses what so many powerful writers of modern fiction lack, a strong and constant sense for narrative. This novel through all its complexities, and its quiet periods of analysis, drives on like the current of a Spring river, gathering in tributaries as it goes, sweeping through backward curves, but always moving at flood intensity. There is not one plot, there are several; there is, one might almost say, no plot to the novel (was there a plot in "Vanity Fair"?) but a theme, the opposition of those whom life accepts and those whom it rejects, which gathers up all plots, all characters, as it goes.

The composition of the picture is simple in the extreme. A

From *The Saturday Review of Literature,* IX (October 8, 1932), 153, 156. Reprinted by permission of *The Saturday Review.*

country girl, well advanced in pregnancy, is seeking the lover who has promised to marry her. She walks shoeless in the warm dust, or rides in friendly wagons, or stays in half willing houses, confidently, because the life force within her makes her confident. And in all this story of murder, rape, lynching, insanity, and remorse, no one hurts her, no one is anything but kind to her, and when even she learns that her lover is worthless, a husband and father for her child, who is not worthless, is provided. She moves with the grain of life.

And all that happens in this novel happens along the road of Lena's story. The fire she sees as she approaches Jefferson is destroying the murdered body of a woman, murdered because her indomitable Puritanism overcoming her lust made her deny herself to her lover, and pray for him. Her lover was Christmas, the victim of mixed blood, the half Negro trying to be Negro, the half white trying to be white, and she was a philanthropist among Negroes whose emotions betrayed her. When the hunt for the slayer begins, headed by Lena's empty-headed lover, Lena herself is brought to Christmas's empty cabin for a peaceful accouchement. And she is delivered of her child by the visionary Hightower who, coming to Jefferson because his grandfather had lived a moment of heroism there, had lost his wife and his church in pursuit of romantic ecstasy. And with her at the birth is the fanatical grandfather of Christmas who thinks himself appointed by God to drive out miscegenation and lechery. And when the ruthless pursuit through life of Christmas by his destiny becomes concrete in an actual chase through backyards and ditches—the manacled victim flying before a youth who has become the symbol of society until he is shot down behind Hightower's table—Lena and her child set out on their way—to Tennessee, or further, what matters —life is with them, not against them.

I shall not try to give a more detailed account of this novel which has the variety of the picaresque and the unity of a "Return of the Native." Byron Bunch, who is to marry Lena, the truckman who sums up the last of the story, the sheriff of Jefferson, Burch the worthless lover, are personality studies, so humorous, so penetrating, and so individual that one welcomes a master of personality. And Hightower, the fanatic grandfather, his macabre and pathetic wife, McEachern who tried to lash the catechism into the boy Christmas whose only moral sensibility was to the problem of his blood, Christmas himself, a tragic figure, are achievements, not so successful as personalities, but impres-

sive, in that different inner world which always lies about and
beyond Faulkner's Mississippi, wretched people, rising above their
terrors into poetic symbolism, or falling below them into fanati-
cism and crime.

I note one great difference in this novel of Faulkner's. His hate
has changed its course. In "Sanctuary" it was concentrated upon
men and women. In "As I Lay Dying" it was the same but mixed
with pity and scorn. In "Light in August" it has made place for
compassion and has fallen, not upon the people, but the land.
Mississippi is hateful—yet, not to Lena. She justifies it, and as
the karma that blacks and whites have made there mounts up and
over the doomed Christmas, and the widow torn between lust and
moralism, and the frightened grandparents who have produced an
evil thing, and the romantic Hightower, and the sullen, secretive
Negroes, the country lives again, becomes possible for human
welfare in Lena and her child.

"Light in August" is by any standard a remarkable book. It will
puzzle many readers, it will shock many readers, it will terrify
many readers if they are honest in their reading. But I think that
no one can deny it the praise of life caught in its intensities both
good and bad, and, without cheap sentiment or melodrama, made
to seem rich, humorous, distressing, thrilling, violent, lovable, dis-
gusting, everything that life is and can be except the imagination
of great minds highly touched which does not enter this book.

I think that Faulkner, like the revivalist preachers, overdoes his
fantasy. I think that his analysis of destiny crushing the unfor-
tunate and yet not letting the sparrow fall is adulterated by the
romanticism of the Fundamentalist preachers he listened to in his
youth. This is in a curious fashion a Methodist book. I think that,
like all the American writers who deal with the vitalities of American experience, he lacks restraint in both style and incident,
probably because he has no precedent for narrative such as his
and must make one. But that he is one of the most powerful,
vigorous, and interesting writers now practising English prose admits of no doubt. Let the skeptic, alarmed by his violence, or
doubtful of his symbolism, compare "Light in August" with the
post-Hardy novels of a roughly equivalent English life. There is
no comparison in originality, force, and intrinsic imagination—
only contrast. This man can go far.

Margaret Cheney Dawson

From "A Rich, Sinister and Furious Novel"

Faulkner's name is one of those that stand for and must inevitably create in the minds of his readers a definite mood, a sort of curious state in which the subhuman is evoked and acknowledged by means of a highly civilized art. "Sinister" is the word that critics always resort to in describing the effect of this process. For Faulkner himself the master word seems to be "furious"; over and over again he uses it, in connections sometimes so unusual that he appears to be belaboring it, himself in a kind of fury, to extract a new depth of terror and anger from it. "Light in August" comes again under the heading of the sinister and the furious, and again, with a noiseless tread, penetrates into the lives of people whose actions lie so close to subconscious promptings that the interval of rationalization hardly occurs at all. Yet the book is not notable chiefly for the mood, the distillation of a dreamlike fear that comes from almost all his other novels. It is a broader, stouter work than anything he has done before. It counts less upon the disembodied emotion, and it is packed, bursting with a mass of detail which explores every phase in the lives of its characters, wandering with leisured and equal insistence over family histories that cover three generations, and individual experience that might take place in three seconds. It would be interesting, and not too far-fetched, to compare it with the novels of Sterne and Fielding, inasmuch as Faulkner seems to be trying, though with a shuttling, intricate disorder that would have pained the eighteenth century, to obtain something of their solidity and richness....

From "A Rich, Sinister and Furious Novel," *New York Herald Tribune Books* (October 9, 1932), p. 3. Reprinted by permission of the W. C. C. Publishing Company, Inc. (formerly *New York Herald Tribune, Inc.*)

George Marion O'Donnell

A Mellower Light

The scene of William Faulkner's latest novel is Jefferson, Mississippi, the locale of four of the six novels that have made him a major writer. And the story is as characteristically Faulknerian as its setting. It will be probably well to warn those to whom "Sanctuary" was distasteful that Faulkner steadfastly holds the view that an artist must not be limited as to subject-matter, must not be restrained by outside pressure from exploring any fields of life toward which he is drawn and which seem to need exploration. For though "Light in August" is more human and less mordant than "Sanctuary," it is decidedly tragic and decidedly unconventional in tone.

Mr. Faulkner utilizes almost 500 pages in the telling of his story. The plot is luxuriant, teeming with a thousand suggestions and implications and complications, but clearcut and lucid at last. As in his other books, Faulkner sheds light gradually upon the events that make up his narrative. There are long flash-backs in which one learns the life history of each of his major characters in turn; and these flash-backs, with their abrupt transitions from the present to the past, from one set of characters to another, give to the narrative a slight looseness that stands in the way of perfection, though it does not impair the cumulative effect of the whole.

The method which Mr. Faulkner has utilized in "Light in August" is interesting. It is simpler than any other he has used in his writing, yet it is a synthesis of all these methods. The author has employed third person, past tense, and present tense narration, the stream of consciousness, first person narration and conversation, blending the various methods that he has used separately in previous books into a whole that is admirably effective if not always smooth. This synchronization gives the impression that Faulkner is striving for a novel-form in which all modes will be blended into a perfect narrative. This perfection is not attained in "Light in August," but it is approached.

In every respect "Light in August" is quieter than the author's earlier works. It is more restrained, less brutal, more leisurely and

From *Memphis Commercial Appeal* (October 9, 1932), Section IV, p. 4. Reprinted by permission of *The Memphis Commercial Appeal*.

dignified in its movement. The author still possesses his power for dramatic, gripping writing about tragic events, and his descriptive epithets are usually so apt as to be startling; but the prose is less staccato than that of "Sanctuary," being more like the prose of "Sartoris" and of portions of "The Sound and the Fury." Even the characters are more human and less pathological than one expects Faulkner's characters to be.

On the whole "Light in August" is a greater work than any other book William Faulkner has written. It is more mature, broader in outlook, nearer to the final, truthful revelation of human potentialities for which the author is striving. It is a novel that no one who is interested in the growth of American literature can afford to neglect. And that William Faulkner is one of the major writers of our generation is proved here anew.

Dorothy Van Doren

From "More Light Needed"

Mr. Faulkner has written four notable novels by now and a number of short stories. An earlier work or two of his has even been resurrected, although less to be read and noted than to be acquired as Faulkneriana. He has been called everything from a young man of promise to a dreadful example of the decadence of American fiction. He remains one of the half-dozen or so most interesting novelists writing in the United States. And at this point, after reading "Light in August," it is sad to have to indulge in a Cassandra-like head-wagging to declare that of the four notable novels the best is still "The Sound and the Fury," which was also the first. . . .

Because the book as a whole by no means measures up to its best moment, it is worth while asking why. One notes that Mr. Faulkner has taken to repeating himself. This is probably inevi-

From "More Light Needed," *The Nation,* CXXXV (October 26, 1932), 402–403. Reprinted by permission of *The Nation.*

table, for when you have included in one novel the sweep of baser human actions from rape to murder, you may find yourself obliged to include them again in the next. And when you write about the same sort of people in the same section of the deep South, you must inevitably bring in the burning battle between white and black, the curse of idiocy, the plague of poverty and cruelty, or be convicted of romantic trifling. Mr. Faulkner also repeats one or two of his contemporaries. His first paragraph might have been in any book by Elizabeth Madox Roberts. The compound, unhyphenated words which blossom more and more frequently in his pages smell like James Joyce. He might well have omitted some of the Reverend Hightower. He has lost something of what was one of his most triumphant talents, an ear for the rich nuances of Southern speech. But these are actually unimportant defects in what otherwise might have been an intensely powerful novel, and is something less. I should guess that the book's major fault is one of method. Mr. Faulkner writes with a kind of understatement, as if a charge of dynamite that was somehow smokeless and noiseless had been set off under one's feet. The resulting explosion is no less disastrous; but there is no fuss. Along with this understatement goes the method of describing in detail what a character does without ever saying what he feels. The reader is expected to derive the feelings from the resulting behavior. Right here I should say was the difficulty. Joe is introduced to the reader as ruthless, lonely, and proud. With the cut-back made familiar to "Sanctuary," the reason is given. And the matter ends there. What is he thinking while he is under the fatal spell of Miss Burden's pitiful lust? What is he thinking when he strolls into Mottstown after a week of having been hunted through the woods with bloodhounds, and stands on the main street until somebody recognizes him? What is he thinking when his own grandmother, he who had no mother or father or child or kin, comes to him in jail and promises him sanctuary? He believes her and runs where she tells him and is shot. But what does he think? What does he feel? The reader should not be obliged to guess, and Mr. Faulkner does not say. One can only wish that he did.

This fault, perhaps of method, perhaps merely a lack of power, effectively answers the claim that Mr. Faulkner is another Dostoevski. What characterizes Dostoevski is a furious, unceasing, passionate ratiocination. The activities of Mr. Faulkner's characters, when the reader is made aware of them at all, take place almost entirely in the viscera. It may be that he does not describe their minds because he is so firmly convinced that they have none. In that case, perhaps a change of locale would help. It is possible that he simply lost interest in Joe Christmas in favor of the Reverend Hightower, which was bad judgment. But if he ever holds himself in with a firm enough hand, and determines that not one drop of feeling shall escape him—or the reader—then it will be time for the wise critics who called him a young man of promise to cash in their checks, with a dividend that will probably surprise them.

F. R. Leavis

Review of Faulkner's
Light in August

Light in August . . . is more readable than the earlier books because in it Faulkner has been much less concerned to be modern in technique. But he has still been concerned too much.

It is his 'technique,' of course, that, together with his dealings in abnormal or subnormal mentality and his disregard of the polite taboos, has gained for him, in France as well as in America and England, his reputation as one of the most significant and peculiarly modern of writers. The technique that matters is the means of expressing a firmly realized purpose, growing out of a personal sensibility. Early in *Light in August* it should have become plain to the reader that Faulkner's 'technique' is an expression of—or disguise for—an uncertainty about what he is trying to do.

There is, for instance, that Gertrude Steinian trick: "Memory believes before knowing remembers. Believes longer than recollects, longer than knowing even wonders. Knows remembers believes" etc. Here it is incidental to a rendering (for the most part in a quite unrelated manner, and one of the best things in the book) of childhood experience. But it is sporadic, applied to various kinds of characters in various circumstances, and it is never

From *Scrutiny*, II (June, 1933) 91–93. Slightly revised by the author. Reprinted by permission of the author.

supported by that minute intimacy in the registering of consciousness which it implies. Indeed, Faulkner is seldom for long sure of the
point of view he is writing from, and will alter his focus and his
notation casually, it would seem, and almost without knowing it.

This pervasive uncertainty of method goes down to a central
and radical uncertainty. If what is apparently meant to be the
central theme of the book, the conflict in Christmas of the white
and the negro blood, had been realized and active, we should necessarily have had somewhere and by some means an intimate and
subtle rendering of his consciousness. But in spite of the technique
and in spite of the digression—for it strikes us as that—back into
childhood, he remains the monotonously 'baleful' melodramatic
villain whose mysteriousness is of so familiar a kind, depending on
our having only a surface to contemplate. Faulkner, in fact, in his
vision of Good and Evil is like Dickens—at his best simple, at his
worst, sentimental and melodramatic. The brutal submorality of
Christmas might have been significant in a Dostoevsky context
and, so, interesting; but when Faulkner, rightly not trusting the
job made of it by his 'technique', pumps in the Significance
straightforwardly at the death of Christmas, its quality appears
in the prose of this:

> 'Then Grimm too sprang back, flinging behind him the bloody
> butcher knife. "Now you'll let white women alone, even in hell,"
> he said. But the man on the floor had not moved. He just lay there,
> with his eyes open and empty of everything save consciousness,
> and with something, a shadow, about the mouth. For a long moment
> he looked up at them with peaceful and unfathomable and unbear-
> able eyes. Then his face, body, all, seemed to collapse, to fall in
> upon itself, and from out the slashed garments about his hips and
> loins the pent black blood seemed to rush like a released breath.
> It seemed to rush out of his pale body like the rush of sparks from
> a rising rocket; upon that black blast the man seemed to rise soar-
> ing into their memories for ever and ever. They are not to lose it,
> in whatever peaceful valleys, besides whatever placid and reassur-
> ing streams of old age, in the mirroring faces of whatever children
> they will contemplate old disasters and newer hopes. It will be
> there, musing, quiet, steadfast, not fading and not particularly
> threatful, but of itself alone serene, of itself alone triumphant.'

There are, as has been implied, good parts. The account of
Christmas's childhood and boyhood is one of these. But it remains,
like so much else in the book, separate, unrelated organically, and

the subject of it is only nominally related to the villain-hero who dies in the passage quoted above. The long history of the family of Miss Burden, the murdered paramour, is also good in its way, and the tacking on is done with an innocent directness contrasting oddly with the pervasive 'technique': "She told Christmas this while they sat on the cot in the darkening cabin."

The Reverend Gail Hightower, another main character, again illustrates the uncertainty of grasp and purpose. He hovers between the planes of Mr. Dick and Miss Havisham, soaring up to the latter (in cheap prose and cheap sentiment) when Significance gives the cue. The old couple, Hines, belong irremediably to the plane of Dickensian-grotesque, but they are solemnly pushed on the stage as tragic actors.

What Faulkner renders with most conviction is the simple-shrewd vegetative mentality of his rustics and small-town citizens (indeed, he finds it so congenial that he again and again uses it, quite improbably and with great technical naiveté, as the medium of presentation). His heart is with his simple heroine and hero, Lena and Byron Bunch, and where they are concerned his sentimentality is not offensive as it is in his flights of high-tragic Significance. The Old South is the strength of his book; one gets intimations of a mellow cultural tradition, still, it appears, in some degree surviving, that recall that great book, *Huckleberry Finn*. But it is too late for another Mark Twain.

3. Critical Essays

Richard Chase

The Stone and
the Crucifixion

Without ado I wish to direct attention to the symbolic texture
of *Light in August*. This texture is very much a matter of mechanics and dynamics—a poetry of physics. Repeatedly Faulkner
presents appearance, event, and even character in the images of
stasis, motion, velocity, weight, lightness, mass, line, relative position, circle, sphere, emptiness, fullness, light, and dark. The phrase
"light in August" has at least two meanings. As Mr. Malcolm
Cowley informs us in his *Portable Faulkner*, the phrase means
"light" as opposed to "heavy" and refers to a pregnant woman
who will give birth in August. And it also means "light" as opposed
to "dark"—an affirmation of life and human spirit. *Light in August*
may be described, in Faulkner's own words (though he is describing something else), as "the mechanics, the theatring of evil." This
is not a complete or fully fair description of Faulkner's novel, but
it is complete and fair enough to demand that we look at the novel
from this point of view—and that we finally ask, How successful
is the author in extending his account of the mechanics and theatring of evil into an account of the human situation?

The reader of *Light in August* will be puzzled in the first few
pages by what may be called "the string of beads image." We read
that the wagon in which Lena Grove rides through the August
afternoon is like "a shabby bead upon a mild red string of road"
and that the village beside the railroad, from which she begins her
long journey, is like "a forgotten bead from a broken string." Later
our attention is called to the row of iron bars in the fence which
surrounds the orphanage of Joe Christmas' childhood, to the identical windows of a street car, to a picket fence, and to the rows of
identical white houses in which the lower-middle-class whites live.
To these images of linear discreteness Faulkner opposes images of
the curve. Lena Grove—searching for Lucas Burch, the father of
her unborn child—passes through "a long monotonous succession
of peaceful and undeviating changes from day to dark and dark

From *Kenyon Review*, X (Autumn, 1948), 539–551. Reprinted by permission
of *The Kenyon Review* and of the author's estate.

to day"; but her mode of action and of consciousness is not of the
order of the "string of beads." She is "like something moving forever and without progress across an urn." For her the road is not
linear but like a string "being rewound onto a spool." These images
of linear discreteness and curve are extended into one of the central images of the book: flight and pursuit.

We have already encountered the symbolic representation of
two realms of being which are counterposed throughout the novel.
The linear discrete image stands for "modernism": abstraction,
rationalism, applied science, capitalism, progressivism, emascula-
tion, the atomized consciousness and its pathological extensions.
The curve image stands for holistic consciousness, a containing
culture and tradition, the cyclical life and death of all the creatures of earth. Throughout the novel, Lena retains her holistic
consciousness and she is strong, enduring, hopeful. All the other
characters in one way or another are victims of the linear delusion.
For Joe Christmas, in whom the linear consciousness becomes
pathological, the curve image is a "cage" or a "prison" to be broken
out of. Or it is something to be gashed from the outside so that
whatever it contains will be spilled meaninglessly out. Joe gashes
the whiskey tins he and Burch have buried in the woods as he has
a vision of trees in the moonlight, standing like "a row of suavely
shaped urns," each one cracked and extruding "something liquid,
deathcolored, and foul." At the end, when Joe can no longer per-
form this symbolic act of even smashing, the curve image becomes
the fateful circle of repetition which he has never really either
escaped or broken and which is the only path to the only kind of
holism he will ever find: death. "I have never got outside that
circle. I have never broken out of the ring of what I have already
done and cannot ever undo." The tragic irony of the linear consciousness, Faulkner seems to say, is that it is an illusion; all consciousness is holistic, but it may be the holism of life (Lena) or of
death (Joe). The remarkable symbol of the wheel in the passage
describing the final madness of the Reverend Mr. Hightower presumably coincides with Joe's circle of doom, though here it may
symbolize the completion in death of a cycle of legendary family
history.

Faulkner's counterposing of motionlessness and motion seems
to imply a fairly consistent deploying of polarity of character.
Lena, Joe, and Hightower each has a certain kind of motionlessness. Lena, "her voice quite grave now, quite quiet," sitting "quite

still, her hands motionless upon her lap," has the inner quiet of
the wheel's axle, a stillness within movement. The stillness behind
Joe's cold, contemptuous mask is the abstract stillness of separation, a schizoid disengagement from outer action. The motionlessness of Hightower, sitting "rigidly" behind his desk, his "forearms
parallel upon the armrests of the chair," is the negation of the will
and action by fear, "denial," and impotence.

The quality of Joe's action is simply a willed translation of his
separateness. Whenever he is in motion, in fantasy or actuality,
he is in flight; and this is true even of his many connections with
women—these also he must turn into the pattern of flight whenever they threaten to bring him too close to the kind of central and
holistic place represented by Lena. Although Burch is throughout
the book in a sense in flight from Lena, Byron Bunch, or the sheriff,
his movements entirely lack Joe's willed abstract control. He is
pure aimless motion, a rural poor white uprooted and cast adrift
in an industrial-urban society. "He puts me in mind," says Byron
Bunch, "of one of these cars running along the street with a radio
in it. You can't make out what it is saying and the car ain't going
anywhere in particular and when you look at it close you see that
there ain't even anybody in it." A friend of Bunch's replies, "Yes,
he puts me in mind of a horse. Not a mean horse. Just a worthless
horse." This rude progression of metaphors will serve to indicate
that Faulkner's imagination very frequently approaches the level
of human character and consciousness beginning with the mechanical, and proceeding to the animal level through an interme-
diate level of dynamics.

The denouement of the novel can be conceived as the final resolution of several kinds of motion. Byron Bunch separates himself
from his spiritual kinship with Hightower and his hitherto meaningless life finds its repose in Lena. Burch moves away from Lena,
dooming himself, as it were, to aimless perpetual motion. The final
flight of Joe to Hightower's house may seem too little explained
as part of the plot. But it has a symbolic significance, since Joe,
turning away for the last time from the realm of being which is
represented by Lena and which he has tried to find in his various
women, finds his ultimate refuge in the castration and death
vouchsafed to him by Percy Grimm (only the last of all the symbolic castrations and deaths he has first sought and then endured).
Hightower himself had turned away from the Lena-holism when
years earlier he had in effect pursued his wife out of existence by

believing in his fantasy that his "seed" had died with his grandfather in the Civil War.

II

  Mr. Robert Penn Warren suggests that Faulkner's objection to
the modern world is that it lacks the ability to set up "codes, concepts of virtue, obligations" by which man can "define himself as
human" and "accept the risks of his humanity." In *Light in August*, Faulkner seems to be concerned with showing that the codes
modern man *does* set up do *not* allow him to define himself as
human—that codes have become compulsive patterns which man
clings to in fear and trembling while the pattern emasculates him.
Byron Bunch, wondering why he lives to the split second by his
big silver watch and works alone in the planing mill every Saturday
afternoon and why the Reverend Mr. Hightower has refused to
leave Jefferson, the scene of his ruin and disgrace, reflects, "It is
because a fellow is more afraid of the trouble he might have than
he ever is of the trouble he's already got. He'll cling to trouble he's
used to before he'll risk a change." Byron and Hightower have for
years been sustaining one another in their "patterns." Their relationship ends over the question of Bunch's aiding and courting
Lena, pregnant with another man's child. The dilemma for each
is whether to stick to a pattern of behavior which prohibits accepting "the risks of his humanity" or to become involved responsibly
in a human situation. Byron chooses to break the pattern and
accept the consequences of intervention. Hightower remains in the
pattern (though he makes certain senile excursions from it),
choosing to conspire in closing the circle of his destiny, choosing
separation and madness. It is not true, as has been said, that all
of Faulkner's characters are rigidly controlled by fate: Byron, for
one, is left free to choose his own fate.

  Joe Christmas is in many ways a masterful portrait of a man
whose earliest years have been spent in an institution—an experience, as the psychiatrists show, which definitively affects not
only the emotional centers of the victim but also the character of
his conceptual thinking. In the forbidding orphanage (a true symbol of the conditions of modern life) Joe finds a surrogate mother
—a cynical, suspicious and indeed almost paranoiac dietitian, a
mockery of the Nursing Mother of the myths. His surrogate father
is an obscenely fanatical inquisitor and peeping tom who functions
as the janitor of the orphanage and who later turns out to be Joe's

grandfather. The pattern of Joe's life is inexorably formed when the dietitian finds that he has been hiding in her closet eating tooth paste while she has been entertaining an intern on her bed (the tube of tooth paste is another urn symbol). The definitive event is not that Joe has seen the dietitian in the act but that she fails to punish him and instead offers him money not to tell. Having felt terribly guilty, having expected and even wanted to be punished, and having had no idea of giving away the secret, he is irretrievably shocked when she offers him the money. He had wanted the woman to engross him in her life, if only by beating him. Instead she denies him this engrossment and gives him a silver dollar, whose shining circumference forms a circle Joe will never break through. Joe's homosexualism is another theme symbolized by the "string of beads" image. The relationship between Joe and his guardian, McEachern, a fanatical apostle of a parochial and degenerate Presbyterianism who beats Joe with the impersonal violence of a machine, has for both McEachern and Joe the uneasy satisfaction of an abnormal but vehemently pure sexual alliance. McEachern has succeeded with Joe where the dietitian failed. Joe finds the relationship "perfectly logical and reasonable and inescapable," and he quickly learns to hate Mrs. McEachern because her proffered feminine kindnesses always threaten to taint an abstract and predictable relationship—just as the food she offers him makes him sick (all the women in Joe's life try to feed him; one of them is a waitress in a restaurant).

Joe's many adventures with women are attempts to escape the abstract quality of a latently homosexual life. As Joe pauses outside Miss Burden's house before keeping a tryst with her, Faulkner says, "The dark was filled with the voices, myriad, out of all time that he had known, as though all the past was a flat pattern. And going on: tomorrow night, all the tomorrows, to be part of the flat pattern, going on." "Then," says Faulkner, "it was time"—which seems to be a pun (the same one occurs in *The Sound and the Fury*) meaning that now Joe's existence can be measured by time (the urn consciousness) rather than by the abstraction of eternity. But the connection with Miss Burden, like all of Joe's connections with women, turns into a ritual reaffirmation that no such connection is possible, a circular path back to the compulsive pattern—as we see when after various ingenious phases of sexual flight and pursuit, Miss Burden, before Joe kills her, is transmuted in appearance and behavior into a mocking likeness of McEachern. The sexual dilemma of Joe's life is nicely symbolized in the episode

where he lolls in the woods (and gashes the whiskey tins) reading
a magazine "of that type whose covers bear either pictures of
young women in underclothes or pictures of men shooting one
another with pistols." He reads as a man "walking along the street
might count the cracks in the pavement, to the last final page, the
last and final word." He goes through life with this same attach-
ment to his pattern, hating the women in underclothes, longing for
a purely masculine annihilation.

In symbolic polarity to the compulsive pattern we have Lena,
who does not need to flee from involvement in human life, and
Lucas Burch. Distantly adumbrating all the polarities of *Light in
August*, the gay, irresponsible, aimless Burch symbolizes pure
Chaos. Perhaps through the child in Lena's womb, Burch symbolizes the undetermined possibility of a future the direction of
which will be decided by the final resolution of forces among the
other characters. If so, we may say that *Light in August* is a "hopeful" book. For the future is in the hands of Lena and Byron Bunch
—a woman who endures and loves and a man who has decided to
"accept the risks of his humanity."

III

Mr. Warren suggests that we ought not to think of Faulkner as
an exclusively Southern writer but as a writer concerned with
modern times in general. To this, one might add that Faulkner has
many affinities with both Hawthorne and Melville. As Malcolm
Cowley has said, the myth of a Southern society which emerges
from Faulkner's work as a whole can be compared with Hawthorne's myth of New England. One might add that the dilemma
with which Faulkner confronts Bunch and Hightower—whether to
take the responsibility of moral intervention in human affairs—is
the same dilemma which confronts many of Hawthorne's characters (for example, the painter in "Prophetic Pictures"). Joe
Christmas would be recognized by Hawthorne; for he is frightened
and obsessed by the inescapable stain on every human life. There
is never any real proof that Joe is part Negro, but Joe's gratuitous
assumption that he is tainted is at the root of all his actions. He
becomes as obsessed with his stain as does Aylmer with the blem-
ish on his wife's face in Hawthorne's "The Birthmark" and with
a purpose as relentless and immoral as Aylmer's he goes about
removing the stain—an impulse which arises in the central figures
of both "The Birthmark" and *Light in August* from what is, in the

final moral terms, simply their inability to bear the burden of being human. (The word "burden," by the way, seems to have the same significance for the Southern writers as the pack of the peddler had for Hawthorne and Melville: the "burden" of one's history or of one's continually self-annihilating humanity. Miss Burden, in *Light in August,* is not the only character in Southern fiction so named.)

Faulkner and Melville share a liking for physical, dynamic, and animal images. Both abound in images of light and dark. In Faulkner's novel there is a persistent reference to white "blood" and black "blood," and Joe's ambiguous character is symbolized by the dark serge trousers and white shirt he invariably wears. Both Ahab and Joe Christmas are seeking an elusive *purity,* symbolized by whiteness. Both shape their doom by their sharp rejections of their own humanity. Both are "unmanned," to use Melville's word, by fate or by their own moral acts. Faulkner's manner of handling symbols and themes is like Melville's. His downright spiritual vehemence often produces a wonderful lyric or epic sense of life; but sometimes the symbols are crudely imagined or imperfectly assimilated in context. For example, the uneasy connection of Joe Christmas with Christ: several of Joe's acts take place on Friday, or "on the third day"; Mrs. McEachern washes his feet; Burch betrays him for a thousand pieces of silver; Hines, his grandfather and the only father Joe knows, imagines that he is God. Faulkner seems not to sense exactly how the Christ theme should be handled, sometimes making it too overt and sometimes not overt enough. His attempts to enlarge Joe's character by adducing a willed mythology remind one of Melville's similar attempts in *Pierre.* It may finally seem to us that Faulkner and Melville are most in control of their work when they approach the epic form, as in *As I Lay Dying* and *Moby-Dick;* but that when they try novels of complex symbolic human relationships, their effort suffers from their uncertain power of grouping symbols into a close coherent statement.

IV

It has been said of Faulkner that his rhetoric and the actions it expresses are so terrific that they annihilate his characters, that his characters become mere targets for violent emotive bombardments. The measure of truth in this criticism does not destroy Faulkner as an artist. It simply indicates that he is one kind of

artist—surely he is not a novelist of manners in quite the way
that such a phrase as "the Balzac of the South" would imply. As
if in self-criticism, Faulkner writes of Hines and his fanatical sermons: "So they believed that he was a little crazy. . . . It was not
that he was trying to conceal one thing by telling another. It was
that his words, his telling, just did not synchronize with what his
hearers believed would (and must) be the scope of a single individual." Yet in one of the utterances of the Reverend Mr. Hightower we find this idea translated into a true definition of tragedy:
"Too much happens. That's it. Man performs, engenders, more
than he can or should have to bear. That's how he finds that he
can bear anything. That's it. That's what is so terrible." In such
a statement as this Faulkner begins to justify the overplus of
superhuman and subhuman violence in his novels. Nevertheless
there remains a discrepancy between the theoretical justification
and the artistic practice. We cannot avoid phrasing the aesthetic
implication of Hightower's words in some such way as this:
"Faulkner attributes more action and emotion to his characters
than can meaningfully be attributed to them."

The alienation of man *via* language is a common theme in *Light
in August*. The people who have beaten and robbed Joe and left
him on the floor of a cheap boarding house, speak "in a language
which he did not understand." The sermons of Hightower seem to
have been expressly contrived to separate him from his congregation. As for Lena, her separation-by-language is always maintained
only to the degree necessary to her total purpose. When she asks
along the road for Burch, people direct her to "Bunch," but to her
they always seem to say "Burch." She is purposefully separated
from irrelevance and relaxed in her vision of reality. Separation
by language is surely a fact of human life. But is Faulkner entirely
in control of this theme? In the orphanage the dietitian and Hines
meet "calm and quiet and terse as two conspirators" and then pro-
ceed to discourse in some pseudo-Old Testament language which
is anything but calm, quiet, or terse. But perhaps it is another
form of dissociation which makes this putatively powerful situation
seem defective. Perhaps—in order that the dissociation might be
in *his* mind, for it needs to be in *someone's* mind—the five-year-old
Joe should have been present, watching and listening in awe to
the terrible creatures, his mythical father and mother. It is simply
a novelist's mistake to present us with a sharp dislocation between
his characters and what they say, without accounting in context

for the dislocation. One feels that Faulkner has missed a chance in this scene to form a profound associative human situation.

This leads us to a general question: What is the quality of consciousness displayed in *Light in August?* Surely, it is not a consciousness which broods over the whole range of action, associating people with each other or with a culture, establishing their manners and morals in a whole containment. It is a consciousness in flight and pursuit, wonderfully aware of fact, the physical and animal fact, wonderfully in possession of extreme emotions and the ecstasy of violence, cognizant too of the tender humorousness of love, and in general wonderfully fantastic and magical. *Par excellence*, it is the American folk-literary consciousness. When it seeks to interpret or enlighten the human situation, when Faulkner breaks off the humorous-tragical flow of rhetorical poetry and ventures an observation on human manners, he is likely to sound naive. He will speak in the manner of the folk proverb: "Yes, sir. You just let one of them get married or get into trouble without being married, and right then and there is where she secedes from the woman race and spends the balance of her life trying to get joined up with the man race. That's why they dip snuff and smoke and want to vote." Or he will attempt a more intellectually formulated observation, with the following unhappy result: "the faces of the old men lined by that sheer accumulation of frustration and doubt which is so often the other side of the picture of hale and respected full years"—What a piece of philosophy! One can hardly help sensing an uncomfortable hiatus between Faulkner's poetic portrayal of manners and his explicit consciousness of them.[1]

Probably the episodes of family and cultural history which accompany Faulkner's account of Miss Burden and Hightower would mean more to a Southerner than they do to me. But especially in the case of Hightower there seems to be a failure of consciousness precisely at the point where we should understand the quality of the association between Hightower and his own history. Hightower has projected his sexual and spiritual impotence back upon a myth of his grandfather. Faulkner goes along with Hightower on this point, assuming too much that a fantasy projected from some center of real causation is the cause itself. He nearly allows Hightower to determine the quality of his (Faulkner's) consciousness. On the

---

[1] But the observations I have made in this paragraph would be substantially less true if applied to *The Sound and the Fury*.

other hand, he is capable of involving Burch in a situation which calls for a degree of consciousness far above what seems possible, and then arbitrarily giving him the necessary consciousness; so that we have a dull country lout whose "rage and impotence is now almost ecstatic. He seems to muse now upon a sort of timeless and beautiful infallibility in his unpredictable frustrations" (the qualifiers "almost," "seems to," "a sort of" are significant). And a moment later we find Burch (so it seems) reflecting that a Negro he is talking with "does not appear to have enough ratiocinative power to find the town." In *Anna Karenina* a dog conducts a humorous and anxious conversation with himself. But unlike the Burch episode, this does not seem in the least out of place, because Tolstoy with his great associative consciousness always gives one the feeling that he knows exactly when and how much to withdraw or extend his mind in the universe of his novel. I do not mean to imply that Faulkner's novel *lacks* consciousness, but only that the consciousness it displays is sometimes unhappily biassed, bardic, parochial, and, in the societal or cultural sense, unmannered. Davy Crockett still screams in the Southern wilderness.

But of course any discussion which compares Faulkner unfavorably with a writer like Tolstoy must not be guilty of the assumption that Faulkner's Southern culture is as cohesive and knowable as Tolstoy's Russian culture was; obviously it is not. And Faulkner's claim to be the novelist of a culture (if that is his claim) must be judged on the basis of his whole work. Nevertheless the evidence of *Light in August*, though it shows that Faulkner is capable of very fine and very extensive and complex fictional constructions, also seems to indicate that he can fail us exactly at that level of existence where the subtle complications of human behavior have to be established. Faulkner works inward from the extremities, from the mechanics and the ecstasy of life. And this relentless, bardic-American bias often makes us wish he would reverse the procedure, that his consciousness would work through human manners into the human character and then outward toward the extremities it can contain or fail to contain. Human life submits itself to die at the hands of the artist so that it may be reborn in art, somewhat as Joe Christmas submits himself to the beatings of McEachern: "The boy's body might have been wood or stone; a post or a tower upon which the sentient part of him mused like a hermit, contemplative and remote with ecstasy and self-crucifixion." One wants to know finally, What manner of man is this *between* the stone and the crucifixion?

V

But it is only one's high estimation of Faulkner which raises these questions at all. Like the author of *Moby-Dick* Faulkner might say of himself, "I try everything; I achieve what I can." In these bad times, a serious venturesomeness must count heavily with us. But it is also a sense of Faulkner's achievement which makes me think him the equal of any American novelist of his generation. Perhaps *The Great Gatsby* is the only novel of the time which can be defended as superior to Faulkner's best work.

In the nineteen-thirties the liberal-progressive culture turned away from Faulkner for many of the same bad reasons which caused it, eighty years before, to turn away from Melville. If our liberal thought now begins to return from its disastrous wanderings of the last decades—that era of the great rejections—and to recover its vitality, it is because it grows capable of coming to terms with Faulkner, as it already learns again to come to terms with Hawthorne and Melville.

Darrel Abel

Frozen Movement in *Light in August*

I. Symbol

Faulkner's *Light in August* does not (except within the arbitrary perspective of any given character in the novel) delineate a single complete action with a beginning, a middle, and an end. For Faulkner's reality, like Bergson's, is a "becomingness"—not static, but dynamic; not formed, but fluid. To Faulkner, "The present

From *Boston University Studies in English,* III (Spring, 1957), 32–44. Reprinted by permission of *Boston University Studies in English* and of the author.

does not exist, it becomes. . . ." [1] According to Bergson, "Reality is mobility. There do not exist *things* made, but only things in the making, not *states* that remain fixed, but only states in process of change." [2]

A writer's insight into this moving reality, his escape from the static and particular into the vital and general, is intuitive. It is the poetic faculty alluded to in "Tintern Abbey," by which "the heavy and the weary weight / Of all this unintelligible world is lightened" and "We see into the life of things." Bergson defines intuition as *"knowledge which establishes itself in the moving reality and adopts the life itself of things"* (p. 227). He contrasts "intelligence," as an effort to know reality by hypostatizing and analyzing it, with "intuition":

> To think intuitively is to think in duration. Intelligence starts ordinarily from the immobile, and reconstructs movement as best it can with immobilities in juxtaposition. Intuition starts from movement, posits it, or rather perceives it as reality itself, and sees in immobility only an abstract moment, a snapshot taken by our mind, of a mobility. Intelligence ordinarily concerns itself with things, meaning by that, with the static, and makes of change an accident which is supposedly superadded. For intuition the essential is change: as for the thing, as intelligence understands it, it is a cutting which has been made out of the becoming and set up by our minds as a substitute for the whole. (p. 39)

Bergson calls artists men who "are born detached," and who have "a much more direct vision of reality" than other men (pp. 162–163).

If Faulkner has, as I think, a similar conception of reality in flux, and a similar theory of the imaginative writer's gift and function, his technique must master a paradox: in order to fix reality in a literary construct, it must freeze movement. "Faulkner appears to

---

[1] Jean-Paul Sartre, "Time in Faulkner: *The Sound and the Fury,"* trans. Martine Darmon, in Frederick J. Hoffman and Olga W. Vickery, *William Faulkner: Two Decades of Criticism* (East Lansing, Michigan: Michigan State College Press, 1954), p. 183. Reprinted from *Situations,* I, "Le Bruit et la fureur" (Paris: Gallimard, 1947), pp. 70–81.

[2] Quoted by permission of the publishers, The Philosophical Library, from Henri Bergson, *The Creative Mind,* trans. Mabelle L. Andison (New York: The Philosophical Library, 1946), p. 222. All subsequent quotations cited by page numbers enclosed in parentheses in the text refer to this edition.

arrest the motion at the very heart of things; moments erupt and freeze, then fade, recede and diminish, still motionless." [3] In Bergsonian terms, the artist's "intelligence" must make "cuttings" out of the "becoming" which his "intuition" perceives: "Our mind, which seeks solid bases of operation, . . . has as its principal function, in the ordinary course of life, to imagine *states* and *things.* . . . It substitutes for the discontinuous the continuous, for mobility stability. . . . This substitution is necessary to common sense, to language, to practical life" (p. 222).

The resource of the intuitive artist in conveying his intuitions to practical men, who must have reality represented to them in "states" and "things," is symbolism. Intuition "will have to use ideas as a conveyance. It will prefer, however, to have recourse to the most concrete ideas, but those which still retain an outer fringe of images. Comparisons and metaphors will here suggest what cannot be expressed" (p. 48). "No image will replace the intuition of duration [i.e., of "becomingness," of "mobility"], but many different images . . . will be able, through the convergence of their action, to direct the consciousness to the precise point where there is a certain intuition to seize on" (p. 195). Although symbolization is the artist's best expedient for communicating his intuitive knowledge of the mobile and continuing reality, it is still only a suggestive makeshift; it conveys no absolute insights, only relative conceptions: *"Relative is symbolic knowledge through pre-existing concepts, which goes from the fixed to the moving"* (p. 227). "Relative" knowledge "depends on the viewpoint chosen and the symbols employed," but "absolute" knowledge (i.e., "intuition of duration") "is taken from no viewpoint and rests on no symbol" (p. 187). Symbolism is merely a means by which "we lean our communication up against a knowledge that our interlocutors already possess" (p. 81).

In *Light in August* Faulkner attempts to contrive through symbols an immobile representation of mobility, and at the same time to suggest how "relative" and arbitrary any distinct and arranged version of mobile reality must be. He endeavors to represent a fluid reality in the static terms "necessary to common sense, to language, to practical life"; and at the same time to disclose that the static images through which he makes the fluid reality visible are merely arrested and discontinuous blinks—what Bergson calls "snapshots" or "cuttings made out of the becoming."

---

[3] Sartre, "Time in Faulkner," p. 182.

Such a symbolic shuttering of reality controls the narration from
the opening pages, which offer an image, immediately augmented
into a symbol,[4] of the mule-drawn country wagons in which Lena
Grove made her enchanted, ineluctable progress from Alabama
into Mississippi; "backrolling now behind her a long monotonous
succession of peaceful and undeviating changes from day to dark
and dark to day again, through which she advances in identical
and monotonous and deliberate wagons as though through a succession of creak-wheeled and limp-eared avatars, like something
moving forever and without progress across an urn." [5]
    In this figure the countryside across which Lena travels is, like
the "silent form" of Keats's urn,[6] a designated image or visible
metaphor of eternity. The stories of Lena Grove and Joe Christmas constitute the "legend" (or "brede" or "frieze") seen against
this immutable image of eternity. A legend is both an inscription
and an old story, especially an "old story" in the colloquial sense
of something happening over and over again from time immemorial.
Against the background of countryside which is Faulkner's equivalent of the "silent form" of Keats's urn, the comic and pathetic
leaf-fring'd [7] legends of Lena Grove and Joe Christmas are seen
to be, although interesting as individual histories, even more significant as expressions, moments, postures, phases of a human
reality into which all personal realities fade. The stillness of urn
and countryside represent, not immobility itself, but "deserts of

---

[4] I use the terms "image," "symbol," and "figure" in this paper in the different senses which I think they usually carry: "image"—a distinct, unified
sense-impression of an object; "symbol"—an image which is the nucleus and
sign of a congeries of not readily explicable meanings and sensations; "figure"—pattern or design, possibly a configuration of images in time or space;
also, any kind of trope.

[5] Quoted by permission of the publishers, Random House, from William
Faulkner, *Light in August* (New York: Modern Library, 1950), Chap. I.
All subsequent quotations cited by chapter numbers enclosed in parentheses
in the text refer to this book.

[6] For more explicit allusions by Faulkner to Keats's "Ode to a Grecian Urn"
which show how persistently Keats's urn-symbol has haunted Faulkner's
imagination, see Faulkner's article "Verse Old and Nascent: A Pilgrimage,"
Double-Dealer, VII (1925), 130; and "The Bear," *Go Down, Moses* (New
York: Modern Library, 1955), p. 297. Norman Holmes Pearson has commented on Keats's urn-symbol as employed in *Light in August* in "Lena
Grove," *Shenandoah,* III (1951), 3–7.

[7] Professor Pearson ("Lena Grove," p. 6) remarks that Lena's family name
(Grove) alludes to the "leaf-fring'd"; probably, despite the change of vowel,
Burch's name also has this reference. That *Light in August* is "a kind of
pastoral" has been noted by Cleanth Brooks in "Notes on Faulkner's 'Light
in August,'" *Harvard Advocate,* CXXXV (1951), 27.

vast eternity"—so vast that in such perspective all particulars and moments are lost.

Faulkner's somewhat peculiar use of the word "avatar," in characterizing the progressive appearances or apparent progress of both Lena Grove and Joe Christmas through space and time, makes their stories legends of arrested human striving like the "brede / Of marble men and maidens" on the urn. Lena "advances as though through a succession of avatars"; Joe, "as in numberless avatars" (Chaps. I, X). The main signification in Faulkner's use of the term "avatar" is of course simply "embodiment." [8] The avatar-figure, which converts personal histories into a mere succession of envisagements of a continuous and moving process of human "becoming," determines the conception of the other characters in the novel too. In Faulkner's sense of "avatar," Hightower's whole inert existence is a kind of prolonged or aborted avatar, in consequence of his belief "that I skipped a generation. . . . I had already died one night twenty years before I saw light" (Chap. XX). Even Byron Bunch philosophically questions his own determinateness as a self, his own identity: *"You just say that you are Byron Bunch. . . . You are just the one that calls yourself Byron Bunch today, now, this minute"* (Chap. XVIII). Faulkner apparently uses the avatar-figure to indicate that a person's sense of distinct and stable identity is simply a hypostatization of the streaming subjective life in which he transiently exists and which his private consciousness defines for him as *his* life.

A less conspicuous device of Faulkner's for indicating that the "fixed" is only an arbitrary arrest of the "moving" is his frequent

---

[8] Thus, for example, Faulkner calls the old mulatto Lucas Beauchamp in *Intruder in the Dust* an "avatar" ("Lucas in ten thousand Sambo-avatars") of the Negro in a position of moral superiority to the white man who has injured him (*Intruder in the Dust* [New York: New American Library, "Signet Books"], Chap. IX). In the "Appendix" to *The Sound and the Fury* which he wrote for *The Portable Faulkner,* ed. Malcolm Cowley (New York: Viking Press, 1946), Faulkner speaks of old Brigadier General Jason Lycurgus Compson II as "now completing the third of his three avatars—the one as son of a brilliant and gallant statesman, the second as battle-leader of brave and gallant men, the third as a sort of privileged pseudo-Daniel Boone-Robinson Crusoe." In the same "Appendix" Faulkner tells of Jefferson's mousy librarian spending "her life trying to keep *Forever Amber* in its orderly overlapping avatars . . . out of the hands of highschool juniors and seniors": the "avatars" of *Forever Amber,* that is, are the whole succession of forbidden sexy novels which titillate feverish adolescent fancy. "Avatar," in these various instances, seems to signify a periodic succession of embodiments of an essentially identical reality—or, as in "ten thousand Sambo-avatars," perhaps multiple simultaneous embodiments.

mention of the omnipresent muted hum of natural life,[9] furnishing
a vague, monotonous, repetitious, generalized accompaniment to
foreground action. Thus Joe Christmas, voicing his finally definite
intention to murder Joanna Burden, heard around him "a myriad
sounds, ... voices, murmurs, whispers: of trees, darkness, earth,
people: his own voice; other voices evocative of names and times
and places ..." (Chap. v). As he entered the house later, to commit the deed, "The dark was filled with voices, myriad, out of all
time that he had known, as though all the past was a flat pattern.
And going on: tomorrow night, all the tomorrows, to be a part of
the flat pattern, going on" (Chap. xii). After Christmas' capture,
as Hightower hears from Mrs. Hines the story of his early life,
"through the open window there comes now only the peaceful and
myriad sounds of the summer night" (Chap. xvi). And later, as
Hightower is alone in his house, struggling to suppress his humane
impulse to sympathize with and help "poor mankind": "Beyond
the open window the sound of insects has not ceased, has not
faltered" (Chap. xvi). These generalized, remote, anonymous
voices of changing, enduring reality constitute an audible image
of the continuous and moving, just as urn and countryside are its
visible image.

If, then, *Light in August* eschews classical form—lacks a single
complete action with a beginning, a middle, and an end—it does
so because there is no alpha or omega in Faulkner's alphabet of
reality. His novel ends, but his story does not: it is merely a harsh
and prolonged suspiration swelling out of and subsiding into the
"myriad voices, out of all time." Faulkner's story is about con-
vergent or connected human destinies, which have as their nexus
the burning of the Burden house, an event which any individual
character views as a fixed and understood reality, but which is in
fact a symbol capable of as many significances as the various
individuals who view it are enabled to read into it from their own
experience, their own ideas. To the stranger who brings Lena to
Jefferson, it is merely "a house burning" (Chap. i). But as a crucial moment in each of the human histories which converge in it,
it is variously interpreted. To each, it brings "light in August" in
a different way, provides a glaring but transient interval of illumi-
nation and realization.

---

[9] Faulkner's "myriad voices, out of all time" correspond to what Bergson
calls "the uninterrupted humming of life's depths" (pp. 176–177). Faulkner
externalizes and objectifies the concept by finding an "objective correlative":
the summertime chorus of insect-sounds.

II. Story

"There is at least one reality which we all seize from within, by intuition and not by simple analysis. It is our own person in its flowing through time, the self which endures" (p. 191). "If, instead of claiming to analyze duration . . . , one first installs oneself in it by an effort of intuition, one has the feeling of a certain well-defined *tension*, whose very definiteness seems like a choice between an infinity of possible durations" (p. 218). The central perception offered to readers of *Light in August* is expressed in Bergson's sentence, "The higher the consciousness, the stronger is this tension of its own duration in relation to that of things" (p. 105). Such a "tension" requires a consciousness of at least two "possible durations": the intuition of our own duration, "which we all seize from within"; and the intuition of some possible duration more comprehensive than our own. Duration consists of "the addition to the present feeling, of the memory of past moments" (p. 211). "The distinction between our present and past is . . . , if not arbitrary, at least relative to the extent of the field which our attention to life can embrace" (p. 179). Thus, intuitions grasp "durations" which vary infinitely in comprehensiveness. They may include awareness of immediate and instant reality, or of our whole lives since birth, or of generations of our family, or of the continuing life of the human species, or of the vast transcendent flux in which the *élan vital* endlessly reshapes reality in novel and more complex forms.

Of the major characters in *Light in August*, the one with least awareness of "this tension of its own duration in relation to that of things" is Lena Grove, for her intuition of her own duration is a very contracted one, and she has no intuition of any other duration. Her "attention to life" embraces only what immediately confronts her; there is little addition to her present feeling "of memory of past events." She cares nothing for her own past or for her family, and never thinks of them; she is fully content with the moment which she occupies, and with the bliss of being in it. As the book opens, she reflects, "*Although I have not been quite a month on the road I am already in Mississippi*"; and as it ends, she says, "Here we aint been coming from Alabama but two months, and now it's already Tennessee" (Chaps. I, XXI). The brief span of her attention to the past is clearly marked in such reflections: the only past she ever speaks of is a very recent one, and she speaks of it only as the antecedent of the present in which she is almost wholly engrossed. Her consciousness has "an inward-lighted quality of tranquil and calm unreason" (Chap. I). "The duration of things" is not measured for her by the tides of God or the clocks and calendars of man, but solely by the elemental urges and responses of her nature to her immediate surroundings. She knows no reality beyond her subjective moment. She represents ordinary naive mankind, inviolably innocent because it cannot enter the realm of ideas. To Hightower she stands for *"the good stock peopling in tranquil obedience to it the good earth"* (Chap. XVII). She is too unsophisticated to comprehend good and evil. Faulkner assigns her the first and last speeches of the novel because, just as hers is the least conscious and sophisticated, so is it the most elemental and enduring, aspect of humanity. She is one of Sandburg's "people who live on," a primitive character like Hardy's "man harrowing clods."

If *Light in August* at all anticipates Faulkner's later statement, in his Nobel Prize acceptance speech, that "man will not merely endure; he will prevail," it does so by identifying the "crucified" Joe Christmas with Lena's child, and by exhibiting her calm and confident onward travel at the end of the story. The hate, mistrust, and evil will which impel mankind to crucify some of its members are counterbalanced by the love, trust, and good will tendered to Lena and her child. Lena prevails, not by her understanding, but by her complacent trust in others, a trust amounting almost to obstinacy and stupidity. Although her story is a comedy of rustic innocence, a comic pastoral, Faulkner dignifies instead of disparaging her.

In contrast, Joe Christmas' story is tragic, or at least pathetic. Although Lena is hardly more than an expression of the will to live of the species, Joe is a person struggling to establish his selfhood, and aware of overwhelming influences extending into his life from a long reach of time and a broad range of human relationships. He saw his own history as a struggle to gain status in white society, or, failing that, to revert to primitivism. A long passage near the end of Chapter v serves as figure for his life. It relates how, on the night before he murdered Joanna Burden, he wandered into the Negro section of Jefferson, Freedman Town, "like a phantom, a spirit, strayed out of its own world and lost. . . . It was as though he and all other manshaped life about him had been returned to the lightless hot wet primogenitive Female." He ran in frantic revulsion "out of the black hollow," but became calm when he reached a white neighborhood with "clustered lights: low bright birds in still-winged and tremulous suspension." He said of the white life around him, "That's all I wanted. . . . That dont seem a whole lot to ask."

As he walked on, he saw behind him "the far bright rampart of the town . . . and the black pit from which he had fled . . . black, impenetrable, in its garland of Augusttremulous lights. It might have been the original quarry, abyss itself" (Chap. v).

In retrospect Christmas saw his career as a vain striving to emerge from the black, primitive, earthy, female, passionate "allmother of obscurity and darkness" (Chap. x) into light, civilization, manliness, volition, identity. In the course of this vain striving, his hatred of the "lightless hot wet primogenitive Female" grew into a complex obsession. His first indelible impressions, at the orphanage, were of females, sex, guilt, and the rejection of Negroes as inflictions divinely and irrevocably decreed. At the McEacherns', throughout his boyhood, these impressions were all confirmed and deepened. His first experience of sex made it for him thereafter simply an overmastering lust: "something liquid, deathcolored and foul" (Chap. viii). After his young innocence and affection had been outraged by the malformed whore Bobbie Allen (an episode grotesquely caricaturing love's young dream), he tried to coerce by injury and hate the world into which he could not find a way by generosity and love. Even at the age of five in the orphanage he had learned to believe that "*I am different from the others*" (Chap. vi), and he never was able to surmount the difference.

After his decisive rejection by the white world, he tried to return to primitive black life. In Detroit

> he lived with Negroes, shunning white people. . . . He now lived as man and wife with a woman who resembled an ebony carving. At night he would lie in bed beside her, . . . trying to breathe into himself the dark odor, the dark and inscrutable thinking and being of Negroes, with each suspiration trying to expel from himself the white blood and the white thinking and being. And all the while his nostrils at the odor which he was trying to make his own would whiten and tauten, his whole being writhe and strain with physical outrage and spiritual denial. (Chap. x)

Christmas failed to recover "the dark and inscrutable thinking and being of Negroes," not because they refused to accept him, but because his upbringing had conditioned him against it. He had not gained a place in the white world, but he had been unfitted for a place in the black world. His was the tragedy of "black blood" in a "pale body" (Chap. xix), an antagonism of two possibilities so equal in strength that each negated the other. Thus Gavin Stevens summed up his tragedy:

It was not alone all those thirty years [of his personal existence] ..., but all those successions of thirty years before that which had put that stain either on his white blood or his black blood, whichever you will, and which killed him. ... His blood would not be quiet. ... It would not be either one or the other. (Chap. xix)

Thus Faulkner shows that the conviction of his outcast fate which dogged "Christmas, the son of Joe" (Chap. xvi) grew in his mind like a fatality. When he anticipated murdering Joanna Burden, he did not acknowledge that he willed to do it, but that he was fated to do it: "*Something is going to happen to me*" (Chap. v). When he murdered her, he "believed with calm paradox that he was the volitionless servant of the fatality [10] in which he believed that he did not believe" (Chap. xii). He transvaluated murder into something like a creative act, however, since it was for him a symbolic annihilation of the world which had denied his claims to selfhood and status. Joanna Burden was his appropriate victim, for she combined in one person the three elements of coercion which Joe had experienced: femaleness, Calvinism, and obsession with color-difference.[11]

Since Christmas could not find a secure life anywhere, his only alternative was to die: to accept and hasten the doom that he thought was determined for him. After the murder, as he looked at his feet in the black Negro shoes that he had put on to throw the pursuing bloodhounds off the scent, it "seemed to him that he could see himself being hunted by white men at last into the black abyss, which had been waiting, trying, for thirty years to drown him and into which now and at last he had actually entered, bearing upon his ankles the definite and ineradicable gauge of its upward moving" (Chap. xiv).

Just as Lena represents the comedy of ordinary life, so does Joe represent the tragedy of extraordinary life. Hated, corrupted, and persecuted from the hour of his birth, he was not only accused of being evil by those who "crucified" him for righteousness' sake

---

[10] Most of the principal characters in the novel (Grimm, McEachern, Joanna Burden, and even Gail Hightower) act as if their wills were determined by some overruling necessity. For an excellent brief discussion of the theme of fatality in Faulkner, see Rabi, "Faulkner and the Exiled Generation," in *William Faulkner: Two Decades of Criticism,* especially pp. 132–134.

[11] For discussion of the conjoined Negro-sex motifs in *Light in August* see Phyllis Hirshleifer, "As Whirlwinds in the South: An Analysis of *Light in August,*" *Perspective,* vii (1949), 237–238.

(Hines in the name of God, Grimm in the name of patriotism and society); he *was* evil, for he had been imbued with all the sin and corruption of humanity; he was a scapegoat burdened with the accumulated evils of his generation. But even his persecutors were not responsible for the tragedy. Although Hines and Grimm were persecutors rather than victims, although Lucas Burch was Judas rather than Christ, all alike were servants of the general and traditional obsessions which assigned their roles in the tragedy. Byron Bunch's opinion about the town of Jefferson's long harassment of Hightower applies equally well to Christmas' "crucifixion": "The entire affair had been a lot of people performing a play and . . . now and at last they had all played out the parts that had been allotted to them" (Chap. III).

III. Coda

"Installed in universal mobility, . . . consciousness contracts in a quasi-instantaneous vision an immensely long history which unfolds outside it. The higher the consciousness, the stronger is this tension of its own duration in relation to that of things" (p. 105). Gail Hightower is the most significant character in *Light in August* because only he attained the higher consciousness which "contracts in a quasi-instantaneous vision an immensely long history which unfolds outside it." Hightower suffered even more than Joe Christmas, for he who experiences most suffers most. Hightower tried to maintain that he had "bought immunity" (Chap. XIII) from involvement in the affairs of living men, but his long-suppressed humanity impelled him "to come back into life" (Chap. XIII) to assist at a birth and try to prevent a death. His identification with the human beings whose fates, when he was forced to sympathize with them, illustrated both the hopeful and tragic possibilities of the life he had evaded made him comprehend the general fate of mankind, which is to serve the compulsive ideas which are its inheritance. Hightower's own story is an exaggerated rendering of the truth that all men are directed by ancestral ghosts and do not fully possess their own realities. He had chosen to withdraw into his ancestral ghost, rather than to let the human past summed up in him enter the present; but his story, like Joanna Burden's and Joe Christmas', shows the persistence through generations of a pattern of transmitted ideas and tendencies which effectually make each inheritor their instrument, because they are not externally dictated to him but are constitutive of his own character.

Because Hightower had so long lived a "dead life in the actual
world," "dissociated from mechanical time" (Chap. xvi), had not
enacted a vital role in the present, he was able, like God in a high
tower in a medieval mystery play, to see that present with detach-
ment. He had breadth of understanding and depth of compassion,
and rose to contemplation of those principles of human action,
those conditions of human life, which are so recurrent in time that
they seem ulterior to time, and "tease us out of thought / As doth
eternity." If, in a naturalistic cosmos, Joe Christmas is Jesus
Christ, Gail Hightower is God Himself. Lena Grove, a pagan gen-
eratrix, is mankind aware of its existence only through participa-
tion in the burgeoning life of nature; Joe Christmas lives and dies
in a world of ideas of good and evil; but Gail Hightower, by his
intuition of "universal mobility," philosophically transcends both
the natural and moral worlds.

The concluding revery of Hightower (to whom light in August
comes more effulgently than to any other character, although all
the witnesses of Christmas' death, like the witnesses of the crucifixion of Jesus, have a half-comprehended enlightenment) shows
him in an instant when "consciousness contracts in a quasi-instantaneous vision an immensely long history which unfolds outside
itself." In his agony of comprehension, of realization, Hightower
sits "in the lambent suspension of August into which night is about
fully to come," and all the faces of the recent past rise before him,
but "not shaped with suffering, not shaped with anything: not
horror, pain, not even reproach. They are peaceful, as though they
have escaped into an apotheosis" (Chap. xx). The figure which
structures his revery is a rapidly revolving wheel of thought,[12] or

---

[12] Faulkner, in representing what Bergson calls "intuition of duration," generally uses cyclic figures. Movement across an urn is of course cyclic movement. Joe Christmas feels that for thirty years he has been running "inside
a circle" (Chap. xiv). Lena thinks of her movement along a country road
as being "like already measured thread being rewound onto a spool" (Chap.
i). This simile is also used by Bergson to suggest the sense of "our own person in its flowing through time" (p. 191): "It is, if you like, like the unroll-
ing of a spool.... But it is just as much a continual winding, like that of
thread into a ball" (pp. 192–193). Richard Chase has discussed the contrasting significances of what he calls "linear discreteness and curve" in
"The Stone and the Crucifixion: Faulkner's *Light in August*," *Kenyon Review*, x (1948), 539–551 (reprinted in *William Faulkner: Two Decades of
Criticism*). I think that his argument, although perceptive and valuable, mis-
carries somewhat because he thinks in terms of the form of Faulkner's cyclic
images, instead of noting that they are essentially images of duration.

consciousness, which slows and stops to focus the static images and characters which perception distinguishes in the continuous, moving reality. But the wheel in rapid revolution is a halo full of faces that "all look alike, composite of all the faces that he has ever seen" (Chap. xx).

In this apocalyptic instant in Hightower's vision the faces of Christmas and Grimm, in mortal life obsessed and murderous opponents, "fade and blend." "Then it seems to [Hightower] that some ultimate dammed flood within him breaks and rushes away. He seems to watch it, feeling himself losing contact with earth, lighter and lighter, emptying, floating. . . . [He thinks,] 'With all air, all heaven, filled with the lost and unheeded crying of all the living who ever lived, wailing still like lost children among the cold and terrible stars. . . .' " (Chap. xx). Thus, for an instant, Hightower escapes from the static and discontinuous appearances which constitute reality to ordinary perception: leaves the temporal world of frieze and legend and enters the eternity of the urn-world itself. When, by philosophic intuition, man is able to "arise from a frozen vision of the real . . . to perceive all things *sub specie durationis,*" "all things acquire depth,—more than depth, something like a fourth dimension. . . . What was immobile and frozen in our perception is warmed and set in motion. Everything comes to life around us. . . . A great impulse carries beings and things along. We feel ourselves uplifted, carried away, borne along by it" (p. 186). In the Dionysian dance of life there comes a serene moment of Apollonian vision.

The climactic symbol of *Light in August,* the lambent wheel which Hightower sees in his highest moment of vision as an image of eternity, is an archetypal symbol whose richness can be best apprehended in comparison with literary parallels. The most obvious is Dante's recurrent conjunction of images of light and a rapidly revolving wheel in the *Paradiso* (e.g., Cantos, i, xii, xxviii), especially the elaborate image of the circle of fire, or rapidly whirling wheel haloed with light, which Dante views in the ninth heaven (Canto xxviii). Dante quotes in connection with this image a passage from Aristotle's *Metaphysics* on the *primum mobile,* the "unmoved mover" which is the center and source of this dazzle of cyclic movement. Similarly, Plato's *Timaeus* designates the stars in their courses as "a moving image of eternity"—a passage which may be the source of the famous opening stanza of Henry Vaughan's poem "The World":

> I saw Eternity the other night
> Like a great ring of pure and endless light,
>   All calm, as it was bright,
> And round beneath it, Time, in hours, days, years,
>   Driven by the spheres
> Like a vast shadow moved in, which the world
>   And all her train were hurl'd.

I think it likely that such reminiscences, whether conscious or not, have contributed to Faulkner's symbol of the haloed wheel of Hightower's vision. If Hightower, like Dante, is regarded as one who, while still in mortal life, is afforded a vision of eternity in all its phases, his experience exhibits something of hell, of purgatory, and of heaven. His inferno consists of his witnessing and participating in the complicated tragedy of human evil and mortality which is consummated in the "crucifixion" of Joe Christmas. His purgatory is the initial stage of his revery after Christmas' death, when finally, in "a consternation which is about to be actual horror," he admits his guilt as an "instrument of [his wife's] despair and shame," while "sweat begins to pour from him, springing out like blood" (Chap. xx). He sees, beyond his own guilt, the determinism which fixed this complicity in evil upon him: "If I am the instrument of her despair and death, then I am in turn instrument of someone outside myself" (Chap. xx). Purged by his abandonment of delusion, his admission of truth, he enters his paradise, his moment of perception of an eternal truth which leaves his stale and corrupt "body empty and lighter than a forgotten leaf and even more trivial than flotsam lying spent and still . . . ; so that it can be now Now" [13] (Chap. xx).

But, although *Light in August* contains a *Divina commedia*, a *Comédie humaine* encompasses it: Lena, the almost primitive embodiment of the human species' persistent effort to seek attachments and find durable satisfactions in local, temporal, and personal terms, is presented to us first and last. Her primacy in the story does not mean, I think, that Faulkner rejects Hightower's vision of reality for her view of it, but rather that he regards Lena's reality as the almost universally and constantly available one, and Hightower's as a difficult, fleeting, and rarely attainable one.

---

[13] Faulkner's "now Now" is a verbal device for signaling the moment of Hightower's passage from a temporal now to the Eternal Now. Compare "yesterday today and tomorrow are Is: Indivisible: One" (*Intruder in the Dust,* Chap. ix).

C. Hugh Holman

The Unity of Faulkner's
Light in August

The nature of the unity in William Faulkner's *Light in August*, in fact, even the existence of such unity, has been seriously disputed by his critics. The debate has ranged from Malcolm Cowley's insistence that the work combines "two or more themes having little relation to each other" to Richard Chase's elaborate theory of "images of the curve" opposed to "images of linear discreteness." [1] Those critics who see a unity in the novel find its organizing principle in theme or philosophical statement—"a successful metaphysical conceit," a concern with Southern religion, the tragedy of human isolation, man's lonely search for community—but they fail to find a common ground for the unity they perceive because they neglect properly to evaluate the objective device which Faulkner employs in the novel as an expression of theme.[2] That

From *Publications of the Modern Language Association*, LXXIII (March, 1958), 155–166. Reprinted by permission of the Modern Language Association of America.

[1] Introd., *The Portable Faulkner*, ed. Cowley (New York, 1946), p. 18; "The Stone and the Crucifixion: Faulkner's *Light in August*," *William Faulkner: Two Decades of Criticism*, ed. Frederick J. Hoffman and Olga W. Vickery (Michigan State Coll., 1951), pp. 205–217. Between these two extremes a great variety of attitudes have been held. Irving Howe, although he praises the novel, feels that it "suffers from a certain structural incoherence" resulting from its use of "a triad of actions" (*William Faulkner: A Critical Study*, New York, 1952, pp. 153, 149). Conrad Aiken feels that it fails because Faulkner's excessive concern with formal technique is not here "matched with the characters and the theme" ("William Faulkner: The Novel as Form," *Faulkner: Two Decades of Criticism*, p. 145). George M. O'Donnell also feels that the novel is a failure "because of the disproportionate emphasis upon Christmas—who ought to be the antagonist but who becomes, like Milton's Satan, the real protagonist in the novel" ("Faulkner's Mythology," ibid., p. 57).

[2] Harry M. Campbell and Ruel E. Foster find unity in the book through an interplay of its incidents in terms of their contribution to "a successful metaphysical conceit" (*William Faulkner: A Critical Appraisal*, Norman, Okla., 1951, pp. 68 ff.). William V. O'Connor believes that it achieves unity through its pervasive concern with Southern Protestant mores ("Protestantism in Yoknapatawpha County," *Southern Renascence: The Literature of the Modern South*, ed. Louis D. Rubin, Jr. and Robert D. Jacobs, Baltimore, 1953, pp. 153–169. This essay is reprinted in an abridged and modified form as Ch. vi of O'Connor, *The Tangled Fire of William Faulkner*, Minneapolis, 1954, pp. 72–87). Jacobs sees the book as centered in the tragedy of human isolation ("Faulkner's Tragedy of Isolation," *Southern Renascence*, pp. 170–191). Carl Benson finds its theme in man's tragic search for community ("Thematic

device is the pervasive paralleling of character traits, actions, and larger structural shapes to the story of Christ. Viewed in terms of this device the novel becomes the story of the life and death of a man peculiarly like Christ in many particulars, an account of what Ilse D. Lind has called "the path to Gethsemane which is reserved for the Joe Christmases of this world." [3] However, that account is in itself perverse, "a monstrous and grotesque irony," [4] unless the other strands of action in the book—the Hightower story and the Lena Grove story—are seen as being contrasting portions of a thematic statement also made suggestively by analogies to the Christ story. This essay is an attempt to demonstrate that such, indeed, is the basic nature of the novel and that it has a unity which is a function of its uses of the Christ story.

I

The parallels between Christ and Joe Christmas, the leading character in the novel, have not gone unnoticed. However, although many critics have commented in passing on their presence, they have usually been dismissed as casual or irresponsible.[5] But the

---

Design in *Light in August*," *South Atlantic Quart.,* LIII [1954], 540–555). In an interesting but largely ignored examination of the novel just three years after its publication, James W. Linn and H. W. Taylor advanced the provocative idea that *Light in August* is a "counterpoint of stories," and said, "Through this . . . device . . . the novelist can, without any distortion of the individual elements of the material, still express his inner vision, his most personal intuitions, not in so many sentences, but in a design, which, like the structure of music, represents nothing but is a sort of meaning in itself" (*A Foreword to Fiction,* New York, 1935, p. 157).

[3] "The Design and Meaning of *Absalom! Absalom!*" *PMLA,* LXX (Dec. 1955), 904.

[4] O'Connor, *Southern Renascence,* p. 169.

[5] For example, Richard H. Rovere says, "Although it seems indisputable to me that some sort of connection [between Christ and Joe Christmas] was in Faulkner's mind at one point or another, I cannot believe that there is much profit . . . in exploring the matter very deeply or in using it to interpret the novel" (Introd., *Light in August,* Modern Library ed., New York, 1950, p. xiii). Richard Chase says, "Faulkner seems not to sense exactly how the Christ theme should be handled, sometimes making it too overt and sometimes not overt enough. His attempts to enlarge Joe's character by adducing a willed mythology remind one of Melville's similar attempts in *Pierre*" (*Faulkner: Two Decades of Criticism,* p. 212). Carl Benson says, "I am not certain as to just how far we may push the Christ-Christmas parallel (which has often been recognized as a troublesome problem in the book)" (*South Atlantic Quart.,* p. 552). Irene C. Edmonds states: "One feels that he had a very definite connection in his mind between Christmas and Christ. The vagueness with which he establishes the connection suggests that the magnitude of his theme was too great for the limits of his imaginative powers to assimilate. . . . One feels that Faulkner, a Southerner, when confronted by the enormity of

publication of *A Fable*, with its very obvious and self-conscious use of Christian parallels in highly complex patterns, forces us to accept Faulkner's concern with the Christ story as profoundly serious, and recent criticism has also shown us that such a concern is not a late occurrence in his work.[6] Furthermore, in a recent interview, Faulkner has talked very directly about the use of Christian materials in *A Fable* and the function that he feels that such material has in a novel. He said:

In *A Fable* the Christian allegory was the right allegory to use.

Whatever its [Christianity's] symbol—cross or crescent or whatever—that symbol is man's reminder of his duty inside the human race. Its various allegories are the charts against which he measures himself and learns to know what he is. . . . It shows him how to discover himself, evolve for himself a moral code and standard within his capacities and aspirations. . . . Writers have always drawn, and always will, of the allegories of moral consciousness, for the reason that the allegories are matchless.[7]

Apparently Faulkner intends to use parallels to Christ as devices to invest modern stories with timeless meanings; and Christian

---

his attempt to liken a man with Negro blood in his veins to Christ, could not find the moral courage to make the analogy inescapably clear. So it remained a suggestion, trailing away into the obfuscation of It-Could-or-Could-Not-Have-Been" ("Faulkner and the Black Shadow," *Southern Renascence*, p. 196). Beekman W. Cottrell's article, "Christian Symbolism in 'Light in August,' " *Modern Fiction Studies*, II (Winter 1956–1957), 207–213, which takes seriously Faulkner's use of Christian materials in the novel, appeared after the present study had been accepted for publication. However, Cottrell's approach, although illuminating and provocative, is so different from mine that in only one respect, indicated in n. 24, would it have altered my case appreciably. Three other studies have appeared since this essay was written, but they would not have modified seriously the reading given here: John L. Longley, Jr., "Joe Christmas: The Hero in the Modern World," *Virginia Quart. Rev.*, XXXIII (1957), 233–249; Ilse D. Lind, "The Calvinistic Burden of *Light in August*," *New England Quart.*, XXX (1957), 307–329; and Alfred Kazin, "The Stillness of 'Light in August,' " *Partisan Rev.*, XXIV (1957), 519–538.

[6] Ward L. Miner, in *The World of William Faulkner* (Durham, N.C., 1952), pp. 139–141; Robert M. Adams, in "Poetry in the Novel: Or Faulkner Esemplastic," *Virginia Quart. Rev.*, XXIX (1953), 419–434; and Carvel Collins, in a review of *A Fable* in *New York Times Bk. Rev.*, 1 Aug. 1954, p. 1, have called attention to Faulkner's use of the Holy Week in *The Sound and the Fury* (1929). George K. Smart has shown that the very early newspaper sketches assembled in *Mirrors of Chartres Street* used materials from the Christ story ("Faulkner's Use of Religious Terms," a paper read before the Southeastern Amer. Stud. Assoc., Daytona Beach, Fla., 26 Nov. 1955).

[7] "The Art of Fiction XII: William Faulkner," *Paris Rev.*, IV (Spring 1956), 42.

allegory, when it appears in his work, may justifiably be viewed as a means of stating theme. Dayton Kohler correctly says, "Faulkner's treatment of Hebraic-Christian myth is like Joyce's use of the Homeric story in *Ulysses* and Mann's adaptation of Faustian legend in *Doctor Faustus*." [8] It is a pervasive and enriching aspect of the total book, and we expect to see it bodied forth, not only in fragments and parts, but in the complete design.

Light in August consists of three major and largely separate story strands, what Irving Howe has called "a triad of actions." These strands are the story of Joe Christmas, his murder of Joanna Burden, and his death, together with long retrospective sections that trace his life in considerable detail from his birth to the night of Joanna's death; the story of Gail Hightower, his reintroduction into life through Lena Grove and Joe Christmas, and his death, together with retrospective and narrative sections on his marriage and his ministry; and the story of Byron Bunch and Lena Grove, of her search for the father of her illegitimate child, and of its birth. These strands are tied loosely together by the accident of time, some interchange of dramatis personae, and by the almost mechanical device of having characters in one strand narrate events in another. Lucas Burch, the father of Lena Grove's bastard child, is Joe Christmas' helper and would-be betrayer. Byron Bunch, Lena's loving slave, is a friend of Hightower, narrates much of the Joe Christmas story to Hightower and is himself the retrospective narrator for a good deal of Hightower's early story. Joe Christmas' grandmother attempts, with Bunch's assistance, to persuade Hightower to save her grandson, and Joe turns to Hightower in the last moments of his life. Hightower assists at the birth of Lena's child, and Joe's grandmother confuses Lena with her daughter Milly and Lena's child with Joe as a baby. However, these links are not sufficient to tie the triad of actions into "a single action that is complete and whole."

A certain mechanical unity is imposed upon the novel through Faulkner's establishing the action of the story in the ten days between Joe Christmas' killing Joanna Burden and his being killed by Percy Grimm. However, the significance of these present actions is to be found in the past, and the bulk of the novel actually con-

---

[8] *"A Fable:* The Novel as Myth," *College English,* XVI (1955), 475. Significantly Faulkner has called Joyce and Mann the two great European men of his time and has said, "You should approach Joyce's *Ulysses* as the illiterate Baptist preacher approaches the Old Testament: with faith," *Paris Rev.,* p. 46.

sists of retrospective accounts of that antecedent action. Faulkner attempts to preserve a sense of present action as opposed to antecedent action by the device of telling in the present tense all events that are imagined to be occurring in a forward motion during these ten days, and in the past tense all retrospective and antecedent events.

Also there are three distinct bodies of material in the book: formal Protestant religion, sex, and the Negro in Southern society. Each of the story strands deals predominantly with one of these matters but contains the other two in some degree. The story of Joe Christmas is centered on the problem of the Negro in Southern society; the Gail Hightower story is centered in the Protestant church; and the sex element is the controlling factor in the story of Lena Grove, her search for the father of her child, and Byron Bunch's love for her. The interplays of these materials among these separate story strands help to knit the parts of the novel into a whole, but these bodies of material and the stories constructed from them find their most meaningful thematic expression as contrasting analogues of the Christ story.

II

The most obvious of the Christ analogues is in the story of Joe Christmas. Faulkner establishes numerous parallels between Joe Christmas and Christ, some of which are direct and emphatic and some of which are nebulous, fleeting, almost wayward. Strange dislocations in time occur; events in Christ's life have multiple analogies and are sometimes distributed over long periods of time. The parallels often seem perverse and almost mocking, yet they all seem to invite us to look at Joe Christmas as a person *somehow like Christ in certain aspects.* Around his birth and his death events are closely parallel to those in Christ's life; in the middle period of his life the analogies grow shadowy and uncertain.

Joe is the son of an unmarried mother, and the identity of his father is hidden from him and from the world. He is found on Christmas day on the steps of an orphans' home, and he is named Joseph Christmas, giving him the initials JC. His grandfather says that God "chose His own Son's sacred anniversary to set [His will] a-working on" (p. 363).[9] When he is five, his grandfather

---

[9] *Light in August* (New York, 1932). All page references are to this edition of the novel. The Modern Readers Series edition, published by New Directions, apparently duplicates the 1932 edition by photoreproduction.

spirits him away by night to Little Rock to save him from the
orphanage authorities who have discovered that he has Negro
blood. After he is returned, he is adopted by the Simon McEacherns, and upon his first entering their home Mrs. McEachern cere-
moniously washes his feet. The stern Calvinism of Simon McEachern represents the accepted religious order of Joe's world, an
equivalent of the Pharisaic order of Christ's, and Joe achieves
what he later senses to be manhood and maturity when at the age
of eight he sets himself against the formal codification of that order by refusing to learn the Presbyterian catechism. He rejects
three temptations: Mrs. McEachern's food and the feminine pity
which it represents; the Negro girl whom he refuses when he is
fourteen; and McEachern's attempt by means of a heifer to pur-
chase Joe's allegiance to his orthodox conventions. He also rejects
food three times, as Robert D. Jacobs has pointed out.[10] Once,
when he is taken into Mottstown at the age of eighteen by his foster father, Joe goes to a restaurant where he meets Bobbie Allen
and begins to learn about the larger world of which he is a part,
the restaurant being a kind of carnal temple and Bobbie and its
owners being priests of that world.

His middle years are cloaked in obscurity, but at the age of
thirty he comes to Jefferson, and there he is first introduced to us
as a man with a name that is "somehow an augur of what he will
do" (p. 29). He is rootless, homeless, "no street, no walls, no
square of earth his home" (p. 27). For three years he works in
Jefferson. At first he works in the sawmill with Brown who is later
to betray him, and Faulkner refers to them as "master" and "disciple" (pp. 40–41). He becomes the lover of a nymphomaniac,
Joanna Burden, who, after reveling for a while in depravity, when
sex is no longer interesting to her, tries to convert him to the
Pharisaic religious order.

Then one Friday night he kills her, striking in self-defense
against her use of a pistol to force him to subscribe through prayer
to her religion. He flees, and he is betrayed, although ineffectually,
by his "disciple" Brown for $1000. On the Tuesday of his week of
flight, the day of Holy Week on which Christ cleansed the temple,
he enters a Negro church and, using a table leg, drives out the
worshippers. On Thursday night, the night of the Last Supper, he
finds himself in the cabin of what he calls a "brother" and a meal
mysteriously appears before him. Jacobs observes that "this Christ

---

[10] *Southern Renascence,* pp. 175–176.

has no disciple except himself and always must eat alone." [11]
Faulkner says, "It was as though now and at last he had an actual
and urgent need to strike off the accomplished days toward some
purpose, some definite day or act" (p. 317). The next morning he
frantically questions to learn the day of the week, and, finding it
to be Friday, sets his face steadfastly toward Mottstown. Although
up to this time he has been walking, he now enters the village riding with a Negro in a wagon drawn by mules. First he gets a shave
and a haircut; then a man named Halliday recognizes him and
asks, "Aint your name Christmas?" Faulkner reports, "He never
denied it. He never did anything" (p. 331). Halliday hits him
twice in the face, so that his forehead bleeds. His grandfather, who,
being a stern Calvinist, speaks for the Pharisees, tries to incite the
crowd to violence, shouting, "Kill him. Kill him" (p. 327). The
mob, however, leaves him to the "law." He is moved from Mottstown to Jefferson, another legal jurisdiction, and the Mottstown
sheriff yields his responsibility happily. In Jefferson he is guarded
by volunteer National Guardsmen, who spend their time gambling.
He escapes from the sheriff in the town square, runs to a Negro
cabin where he steals a pistol, and then runs to the home of the
ex-minister Hightower, where he is shot by the leader of the
Guardsmen, a self-important soldier. As he is dying, the Guards-
man takes a knife and mutilates him, so that "from out the slashed
garments about his hips and loins the pent black blood seemed to
rush like a released breath" (p. 440). And Joe Christmas, at thirty-
three, as Gail Hightower had earlier prophesied that he would,
becomes "the doomed man ... in whose crucifixion [the churches]
will raise a cross" (p. 348).

These parallels have been dismissed as insignificant, I believe,
because critics have looked for a theological Saviour, whose death
becomes an effective expiation for man's guilt, and viewed in these
terms Joe Christmas is a cruel and irreverent travesty on Christ.
However, Faulkner has defined the function of allegory to be a
chart against which man can measure himself and learn "to know
what he is." And Christian allegory uses Christ as "a matchless
example of suffering and sacrifice and the promise of hope" (*Paris
Rev.*, p. 42). The Christ to whom Faulkner parallels Joe Christmas
is not the Messiah of St. Paul's epistles but the suffering servant
of Isaiah, who is described thus:

---

[11] Ibid., p. 176.

he hath no form nor comeliness; and when we shall see him, there
is no beauty that we should desire him.

He is despised and rejected of men; a man of sorrows, and ac-
quainted with grief: and we hid as it were our faces from him; he
was despised, and we esteemed him not. . . .

He was oppressed, and he was afflicted, yet he opened not his
mouth: he is brought as a lamb to the slaughter, and as a sheep
before her shearers is dumb, so he openeth not his mouth.

He has taken from prison and from judgment: and who shall
declare his generation: for he was cut off out of the land of the living: for the transgression of my people was he stricken. (Isaiah
liii.2–3, 7–8)

III

The central fact in this story of the suffering servant Joe Christmas is his belief that he bears an imperceptibly faint strain of
Negro blood, an ineradicable touch of evil in the eyes of the society
of which he is a part and in his own eyes as well. This Negro blood
exists for him as a condition of innate and predetermined darkness,
a touch of inexorable original sin, a burden he bears neither
through his own volition nor because of his own acts. In the lost
central years of his life his sense of this innate damnation leads
him to shock his many women with confessions of his Negro blood
(p. 211). At last he finds a woman who is not shocked.

She said, "What about it? . . . Say, what do you think this dump is,
anyhow? The Ritz hotel?" Then she quit talking. She was watching
his face and she began to move backward slowly before him, staring
at him, her face draining, her mouth open to scream. Then she did
scream. It took two policemen to subdue him. At first they thought
that the woman was dead.

He was sick after that. He did not know until then that there were
white women who would take a man with a black skin. He stayed
sick for two years. (p. 212)

It is from this aspect of himself that Joe runs in such fatal and
precipitant flight down "the street which was to run for fifteen
years" (pp. 210, 213).

Hightower equates this Negro blood in Joe to "poor mankind"
(p. 93); and Joe, running from the Negro quarter of the town, sees
it as the "black pit," and thinks, "It just lay there, black, impenetrable. . . . It might have been the original quarry, abyss itself" (p. 108). It is this black blood that stands between Joe and

a natural life. It is his own knowledge of it that stands between him and his becoming "one with loneliness and quiet that has never known fury or despair" (p. 313). And it is this black blood which, in Joanna Burden's impassioned view of the "doom and curse" of the Negro, casts a "black shadow in the shape of a cross" (p. 239).

Gavin Stevens believes that Joe Christmas' actions, after he escapes in the town square, were the results of a series of conflicts between his black blood, which is a form of evil, and his white blood, which represents his humane and good impulses. This conflict reaches its climax when the black blood leads him to strike the minister to whom he had run for help, but, Stevens says:

> And then the black blood failed him again, as it must have in crises all his life. He did not kill the minister. He merely struck him with the pistol and ran on and crouched behind that table and defied the black blood for the last time, as he had been defying it for thirty years. He crouched behind that overturned table and let them shoot him to death, with that loaded and unfired pistol in his hand. (p. 425) [12]

After Percy Grimm shoots Joe down, he mutilates him, and then, with the crowd watching, "the pent black blood" rushes from him. Faulkner says:

> It seemed to rush out of his pale body like the rush of sparks from a rising rocket; upon that black blast the man seemed to rise soaring into their memories forever and ever. They are not to lose it, in whatever peaceful valleys, beside whatever placid and reassuring streams of old age, in the mirroring faces of whatever children they will contemplate old disasters and newer hopes. It will be there, musing, quiet, steadfast, not fading and not particularly threatful, but of itself alone serene, of itself alone triumphant. (p. 440)

This is Joe Christmas' crucifixion and his ascension, and this outrushing and ascending stream of black blood becomes his only successful act of communion with his fellowmen. Through it, a symbol of his Negro qualities shed for sexual reasons in the house of a man of religion, Joe Christmas becomes one of "the charts

---

[12] Irene C. Edmonds' objection that Faulkner is here indulging in the fallacious "tragic mulatto" theme (*Southern Renascence,* pp. 196–197) seems justified. However, it seems also true that Faulkner's use of "black blood" has here transcended the level of racial qualities, whether true or false, and has been universalized to all mankind.

against which [man] measures himself and learns to know what he is ... a matchless example of suffering and sacrifice ..." (*Paris Rev.*, p. 42).

Joe's life is also shaped by sexual distortions, perversions, and irregularities. His mother was unmarried; his grandfather's righteous anger at her impurity and at what he believes to be the Negro blood in Joe's father makes him kill Joe's father and refuse his mother the medical assistance which would have prevented her death at his birth. Thus this anger sends Joe into the world an orphan. His accidental witnessing of the illicit relations between an orphanage dietician and an interne results in the dietician's learning of his Negro blood and in his being adopted by the McEacherns. At fourteen, when Joe's turn comes in a group assignation with a Negro girl, he is repelled by the "womanshenegro" and it is against "She" that he struggles and fights, until "There was no She at all" (pp. 146–147). Significantly this early sexual experience is allied in Joe's mind with the Negro.

The menstrual period becomes for him a symbol of darkness and evil. Learning about it from boys' conversation, "he shot a sheep. ... Then he knelt, his hands in the yet warm blood of the dying beast, trembling. ... He did not forget what the boy had told him. He just accepted it. He found that he could live with it, side by side with it" (p. 174). This blood sacrifice he is to duplicate himself in his death. But three years after killing the sheep, when he confronts the idea again in connection with Bobbie Allen, it fills him with horror. "In the notseeing and the hardknowing as though in a cave he seemed to see a diminishing row of suavely shaped urns in moonlight, blanched. And not one was perfect. Each one was cracked and from each crack there issued something liquid, deathcolored, and foul" (pp. 177–178). This image of the urn is to appear crucially in each of the major story strands.

Woman thus becomes for Joe a symbol and source of darkness and sin, the dark temptress who is viewed with revulsion alternating with attraction. Joseph Campbell expresses such a duality in attitudes toward women in terms that might have been designed to define Joe's feeling when in his study of religion and mythology he says:

Generally we refuse to admit within ourselves or within our friends, the fullness of that pushing, self-protective, malodorous, carnivorous, lecherous fever which is the very nature of the organic cell. ...

But when it suddenly dawns upon us, or is forced to our attention, that everything we think or do is necessarily tainted with the odor of the flesh, then, not uncommonly, there is experienced a moment of revulsion: life, the acts of life, the organs of life, woman in particular as the great symbol of life, become intolerable.[13]

Simon McEachern's harsh and grimly puritan ideal of chastity drives Joe to the prostitute Bobbie Allen, appropriately named for the hard-hearted heroine of the Southern folk version of the Scotch ballad "Barbara Allen." [14] And this cheap and cruel woman is Joe's closest approach to love and acceptance, and she at last turns upon him, screaming against his Negro blood.

This pattern of unhappy if not unnatural sex reaches its climax for Joe Christmas with the puritanical nymphomaniac Joanna Burden. In a sense, the ministry that Joe performs during his three years in Jefferson is to call to life in this cold, barren woman the primitive sex urge; as he expresses it, "At least I have made a woman of her at last" (p. 223). But what he awakens in her is not a natural urge, but an unnatural and perverted one, for she was too old to bear children, too old to serve the purposes of nature. Faulkner says, "Christmas watched her pass through every avatar of a woman in love.... He was aware of ... the imperious and fierce urgency that concealed an actual despair at frustrate and irrevocable years.... It was as though he had fallen into a sewer" (pp. 244, 242). Having perverted his "ministry," she finally denies it and attempts to force him into her sterile religious patterns. It is then that he kills her in an act of self-defense, for she had tried to shoot him; and in an act of spiritual self-preservation, for he could live only by refusing to pray with her; but in an act of suicide, for he could not himself long survive her killing.

It is in the Joanna Burden episode that the sex material of the Joe Christmas story reaches its fullest statement. It is in her episode, too, that the union of this material with the idea of Joe's Negro blood is most clearly stated, for Joanna is the daughter of a Northern father in a Southern town. From her childhood she had been taught that the Negroes were "A race doomed and cursed to be forever and ever a part of the white race's doom and curse for

---

[13] Joseph Campbell, *The Hero With A Thousand Faces* (New York, 1956), pp. 121–122. It is this aspect of Faulkner's work that seems to bother Edith Hamilton most in her "Faulkner: Sorcerer or Slave?" *Sat. Rev.,* xxxv (12 July 1952), 8–10, 39–41.

[14] See headnote and text, "Barbey Ellen," in Willard Thorp, *A Southern Reader* (New York, 1955), pp. 618–620, for this ballad in its Southern version.

its sins" (p. 239) and that "in order to rise, you must raise the
shadow with you ... the curse of the white race is the black man
who will be forever God's chosen own because He once cursed
Him!" (p. 240). She first befriends Joe because he is a Negro. And
when the flames of her sexual desires die out she wishes to send
him to law school and to have him administer her numerous chari-
ties for Negro people, but this involves an acceptance of his Negro
status, and such acceptance is intolerable to Joe.

Joanna serves adequately to link these two matters, sex and the
Negro, to religion, for she is a conventionally devout person, and
when she attempts to shoot Joe, thus forcing him to kill her, it is
because he refuses to join her in her return to religion through
prayer.

The formal Protestant religion, an aspect of which Joanna represents, has been haunting Joe from before his birth. His grandfather Eupheus Hines is a half-mad religious zealot with a special
and spiteful hatred of women, of what he calls "abomination and
bitchery." He believes that God speaks directly to him, telling him
how to execute His vengeance on earth. In the narrow, vindictive,
cruel God to whom Eupheus listens may be seen the primitive
Protestant Old Testament Jehovah of anger and jealousy. The
Negro has been singled out for the special wrath of this God, and
Hines goes about as a quasi minister to Negro congregations
preaching to them of God's disfavor. He becomes a kind of perverted and evil divine father for Joe, and he pursues passionately
his desire to destroy his grandson. Although his religion is unor-
ganized and brutally primitive, he seems to speak on the lowest
level of the religious order and attitudes of Joe's world.

Simon McEachern, Christmas' foster father, into whose hands
he is committed when he passes from the orphanage and Hines's
control, is a Presbyterian elder. He attempts to instill through grim
authority the cheerless pattern of Calvinistic conduct and belief.
His only weapon is the flail, and to him love is a deplorable weak-
ness. The crucial occurrence in Joe's relationship with him comes
when McEachern attempts unsuccessfully to force Joe to learn the
Presbyterian catechism. Finally Joe strikes McEachern down in
murderous rage when his foster father comes between him and the
closest thing he has known to love, Bobbie Allen.

When Joe is running away after killing Joanna, he re-enacts
Christ's cleansing of the temple by interrupting a Negro church
service and driving out the worshippers with a table leg. His grandmother, anxious to give him a respite from the punishment he is to

suffer, turns to the disgraced Presbyterian minister Hightower and asks him to give Christmas an alibi for the time of Joanna's murder. She tells Joe to go to the minister. When he escapes in the town square, he turns first to a Negro cabin and then to Hightower, but he strikes the minister down, as he has struck down the others who have symbolized church to him.

Significantly, organized religion is represented by the Presbyterian Church rather than the Baptist or the Methodist, both of which are numerically superior to the Presbyterian in Faulkner's country.[15] Yet Faulkner is remarkably ignorant of the government and instruction of that church. He gives it an episcopal government quite contrary to the government by elders from which it gains its name (pp. 456–457).[16] He seems naïvely ignorant of how the catechism is learned, for he has Joe Christmas standing silent with the book in his hands, as though the catechism were a litany to be recited rather than a group of answers to be repeated to questions (pp. 137–146). However, the Presbyterian Church is the doctrinal church of the Protestant sects, the church of unrelenting Calvinism.[17] As such, it represents the Pharisaic order and is an example of what man does in codifying into cold ritual and inhumane form the warm and living heart of religion.

It is against the dead order of his world as it is defined by this formal religion that much of Joe's rebellion is directed. He defines himself by rebellion against McEachern's catechism and grim and inhumane morality, against Joanna Burden's attempt to force him into her religious patterns, against a symbol of the organized church when he strikes out in flailing anger against the Negro congregation, and against the ex-minister Hightower when he strikes him down. He is pursued and harried by the organized church of his day in a way suggestive of that in which Christ was pursued and harried by the Pharisees.

Joe Christmas is like Christ, so many of whose characteristics his creator has given him, in that he bears our common guilt, symbolized by his Negro blood, that he is denied by the world, and that he is ultimately offered as a blood sacrifice because of the "original sin" he bears. But he is not Christ; he is a rebelling and

---

[15] *The 1936 Census of Religious Bodies,* Bureau of the Census (Washington, 1941), I, 234–237, shows for Mississippi 150,000 communicants in the Southern Baptist Church, 322,362 in the Negro Baptist Church, 107,245 in the Methodist Church, and only 18,445 in the Presbyterian Church.
[16] See ibid., II, 1382, 1402–1403.
[17] Ibid., II, 1402–1403, and esp. p. 1444.

suffering creature, embittered, angry, and almost totally lacking
in love. In his ineffectual death is no salvation. His is a futile and
meaningless expiation of his "guilt."

IV

The religious subject matter is pervasive in *Light in August.*
The sounds of church bells and of choirs echo throughout the novel,
and it is shaped in part by the Protestantism of the South; but
the Gail Hightower story strand is the one most completely,
although by no means exclusively, drawn from this subject matter.

Hightower is the grandson of a Confederate soldier killed in a
raid in Jefferson during the Civil War. He is the son of a pacifist,
an abolitionist, a "phantom ... who had been a minister without
a church and a soldier without an enemy, and who in defeat had
combined the two and become a doctor, a surgeon" (p. 449). Hightower goes to the seminary seeking an asylum from the world and
a means of rejoining his grandfather's ghost at Jefferson.

> He believed with a calm joy that if ever there was shelter, it would
> be the Church; that if ever truth could walk naked and without
> shame and fear, it would be in the seminary. When he believed
> that he had heard the call it seemed to him that he could see his
> future, his life, intact and on all sides complete and inviolable, like
> a classic and serene vase, where the spirit could be born anew shel-
> tered from the harsh gale of living and die so, peacefully, with only
> the far sound of the circumvented wind ... (p. 453)

This "classic and serene vase ... intact and inviolable" is in contrast to the urn with cracked sides and deathcolored fluid which
Joe Christmas imagined he saw when the revolting animal facts of
reproduction were forced upon him.

While in seminary, Hightower marries a girl who is desperately
seeking escape from her life as the daughter of one of the seminary
teachers. He marries her because he quite correctly believes that
she has sufficient influence with the authorities in the church to
get for him a call to Jefferson. But once he reaches Jefferson he
proves ineffectual in every sense. His sermons are half-mad rhap-
sodies on the last cavalry charge of his grandfather. The members
of his church protest that he is using "religion as though it were a
dream" (p. 56). His church and his wife, along with everything in
the present, seem to him to be meaningless, held in suspension,
while reality is "the wild bugles and the clashing sabres and the

dying thunder of hooves" (p. 467). So that, like that other solipsist
in Allen Tate's poem,

> You hear the shout [of brave men at war]—the crazy
>   hemlocks point
> With troubled fingers to the silence which
> Smothers you, a mummy, in time.[18]

His frustrated wife is driven into a pattern of promiscuity which
culminates in her suicide and in his being shut out in disgrace from
his church. But he lives on in Jefferson a flaccid, fat, breathing
corpse. Although the possibilities of an effective ministry for him
have long since passed, he remains a symbol of the church and its
truth to the simple religious man, Byron Bunch.

He is called back to an actual ministry to man by Bunch when
that man sends him to help Lena in childbirth and he has to de-
liver the baby. He is asked by Bunch and by Joe's grandmother to
reassume his ministry by championing Joe's cause and giving him
an alibi. As Byron introduces the request, he apologizes and yet
insists, "But you are a man of God. You cant dodge that." Hightower protests, "I am not a man of God," and he argues that the
town and the church had chosen that he should not be; but Byron
answers, "You were given your choice before I was born, and you
took it. . . . That was your choice. And I reckon them that are good
must suffer for it the same as them that are bad" (pp. 344–345).
At the last moment, Hightower attempts to do what Byron and
Mrs. Hines have asked and to save Joe by telling the lie, but the
attempt is vain, for when Joe, escaping, turns to him, it is with
raised pistol to strike him down. Yet Hightower has been given by
these actions a sufficiently clear vision of the way in which he has
betrayed his ministry for him to understand himself in the moments before he dies. Christmas is for him, indeed, the chart
"against which he measures himself and learns to know what he is."

In the senses that Hightower accepts a "call" to the ministry
not as a field of service but as a sanctuary from the "harsh gale of
living"; that he is absorbed in the past rather than the present—a
past appropriately, for a Southern minister, built on a false view
of Confederate heroism (the cavalry charge is a hen-house raid)—
that his aloofness prevents his ministering to suffering mankind;

---

[18] "Ode to the Confederate Dead," ll. 53–55.

that he has a sharp sense of the ethical values in the human situation (he can properly instruct Byron, for example) but lacks the human sympathy that would make him act on his knowledge—in these senses, he exemplified qualities which Faulkner sees in religion. In Hightower's dying vision of truth:

> He sees himself a shadowy figure among shadows . . . believing that he would find in that part of the Church which most blunders, dream-recovering, among the blind passions and the lifted hands and voices of men, that which he had failed to find in the Church's cloistered apotheosis upon earth . . . [He sees] that that which is destroying the Church is not the outward groping of those within it nor the inward groping of those without, but the professionals who control it and who have removed the bells from its steeples . . . He seems to see the churches of the world like a rampart, like one of these barricades of the middleages planted with dead and sharpened stakes, against truth and against that peace in which to sin and be forgiven which is the life of man. (p. 461)

Hightower is here seeing himself and his failure as microcosmic patterns of the failure of the religious spirit in his world. His is not the harsh failure of understanding or vision which the institutional church can sometimes represent and which is shown in this novel in McEachern and Eupheus Hines; for Hightower had known the meaning of the church and of its call to service: "He had believed in the church, too, in all that it ramified and evoked" (p. 453). But this vision has been smothered by his retreat from a positive engagement in life. One evening, listening to the organ music from the Sunday evening prayer meeting, he broods:

> The organ strains come rich and resonant through the summer night, blended, sonorous, with that quality of abjectness and sublimation, as if the freed voices themselves were assuming the shapes and attitudes of crucifixions, ecstatic, solemn, and profound in gathering volume. Yet even then the music has still a quality stern and implacable, deliberate and without passion so much as immolation, pleading, asking, for not love, not life, forbidding it to others, demanding in sonorous tones as though death were the boon, like all Protestant music. . . . Listening, he seems to hear within it the apotheosis of his own history, his own land, his own environed blood . . . (p. 347)

Malcolm Cowley has noted Faulkner's tendency to turn Freudian method backward, producing "sexual nightmares" that are in reality symbols on another level,[19] and in the story of Gail High-tower that method is well illustrated. As in a sense the "ministry" of Joe Christmas in Jefferson may be viewed as sexual, so in a more pronounced sense the ministry of Hightower is pictured through sexual parallels: the story of his marriage is in miniature the story of his religious failure.

Hightower is impotent. Faulkner says of him, "[It was] as though the seed which his grandfather has transmitted to him had been on the horse too that night and had been killed too" (p. 59), and he instinctively is drawn to Tennyson's poetry, which, Faulkner says, is "like listening in a cathedral to a eunuch chanting in a language which he does not even need to not understand" (p. 301). He marries, not for the love of his wife, but to use her to secure the pastorate at past-haunted Jefferson, and she is driven to destruction by his impotence and neglect. He fails equally the church which he neglects her to serve, and in his dying moments he realizes that these two failures are in truth the same one. He says:

> I served it [the church] by using it to forward my own desire. I came here where faces full of bafflement and hunger and eagerness waited for me, waiting to believe; I did not see them. Where hands were raised for what they believed that I would bring them; I did not see them. I brought with me one trust, perhaps the first trust of man, which I had accepted of my own will before God [i.e., his duty to his wife]; I considered that promise and trust of so little worth that I did not know that I had even accepted it. And if that was all I did for her, what could I have expected? what could I have expected save disgrace and despair and the face of God turned away in very shame? Perhaps in the moment when I revealed to her not only the depth of my hunger but the fact that never and never would she have any part in the assuaging of it; perhaps at that moment I became her seducer and her murderer, author and instrument of her shame and death. (pp. 461–462)

One of man's basic duties is to the natural order of things, a duty to the race and its propagation. On the one occasion when High-tower works in harmony with that natural order and not against it, on the occasion of his assisting at the birth of Lena's son, he experiences a sudden rejuvenation, a sense of strength and right-ness, and he puts away his Tennyson for the redder meat of Shake-speare's *Henry IV* (pp. 382–383). And in his vision of truth he sees

---

[19] *Portable Faulkner*, p. 15.

man's duty to propagate the race as his "first trust," a duty so elemental that a failure here is a total failure (p. 462).

The stories of Christmas and Hightower are counterparts of the same story, but with reversed roles for the characters. The parallels of Gail Hightower to Joanna Burden are marked. Both are the entangled victims of the heroic past, even to the point of both being the descendants of abolitionists. Both are practically sterile; both destroy those in intimate physical relation to them; both follow religions inadequate to meet their actual problems; both represent distortions and perversions of the natural order as it is represented by normal sexual life and reproduction.

Joe Christmas in his self-destructive relation to Joanna Burden has a parallel role to that of Hightower's doomed wife. Both represent comparatively normal basic urges; both are in quite emphatic ways the victims of the impotence of those to whom they are attached; both are offered religious solace, Mrs. Hightower by the women of the church and Joe by Joanna's attempt to convert him; both reject such solace and elect death.

Thus the stories of Joe Christmas and Joanna Burden and of Gail Hightower and his wife become contrasting personal and institutional aspects of the religious aspirations and frustrations of man, as symbolized by deviations from the sexual norm. Ward Miner is only partly correct when he says, "In *Light in August* the force which destroys Christmas, Hightower, and Miss Burden is institutional Christianity." [20] For Joanna Burden is a destroyer rather than a victim, and she destroys through the same atrophy of natural feeling that has ruined the church as institution. Furthermore, Hightower is a symbol of the atrophy of the religious spirit, a figure indicating how and why the churches fail, rather than a victim of such failure. He is withdrawn from life, remote, indifferent; Faulkner speaks of "his dead life in the actual world" (p. 346).

These stories are finally merged, in a plot sense, near their conclusions by Joe's turning to Hightower, and they then stand as contrasting and complementary portions of the novel—contrasting in that the roles of the actors are reversed and complementary in that both are stories of "suffering and sacrifice" and of the failure of man to find and execute what Faulkner calls "his duty inside the human race" (*Paris Rev.*, p. 42).

---

[20] *World of William Faulkner,* p. 143.

V

The stories of Lena Grove and Byron Bunch form more than a pastoral idyll within which the violence of the other stories plays itself out. They establish a norm for the other actions, a definition of the natural order against which the perversions and distortions of the other stories are to be set. Here it is sex which is the principal subject matter.

Lena Grove in her calm and tranquil way is seeking Lucas Burch, the father of her child whose birth is imminent. Traveling alone in the confident belief that he is waiting for her, she arrives in Jefferson on Saturday morning, the first day of Joe Christmas' flight. At the sawmill to which she has been directed she meets a good, devout, earnest man, Byron Bunch, whose name is a Southern colloquialism for "crowd" or "masses." He immediately recognizes that Burch is "Brown," Joe Christmas' partner and now would-be betrayer, and he decides to shield her from a knowledge of the murder and of who Burch is. Bunch seems to possess on a primitive and unthinking level that aptitude for religious sentiment which Hightower betrays. He and Hightower can talk together, and Hightower has been his religious mentor. He shares with Hightower, too, a desire to retreat from the evils of the world. He is working on Saturday in order to escape temptation; when Lena comes, he says, "Out there where I thought the chance to harm ere a man or woman or child could not have found me. And she hadn't hardly got there before I had to go and blab the whole thing [that Burch was in Jefferson]" (p. 284). But Bunch falls hopelessly and completely in love with Lena, and thus he involves himself increasingly in the problems from which he had been fleeing and attempts to involve Hightower too. He sees that Hightower is present to assist at the birth of the baby, sees that the sheriff sends Burch to the cabin to be confronted by Lena and their son, and learns, since he loves Lena, that the fact of that son certifies the other and antecedent fact of Lucas Burch: "Then he heard the child cry. Then he knew ... that there had been something all the while which had protected him against believing, with the believing protected him. ... he thought ... *she is not a virgin. ... It aint until now that I ever believed that ... there ever was a Lucas Burch*" (p. 380). But Byron, learning to face the evil he has been fleeing, faces it completely because he loves Lena. When Burch flees from Lena's cabin, Byron confronts him at the railroad tracks and fights him although the conflict is hopeless. Thus he earns the right to go with Lena, like another Joseph going with Mary, as she continues her journey on into Tennessee, but without real hope of other pleasures than those of serving her.

Lena Grove herself is almost an earth-mother symbol. She moves with tranquil ease and unflagging faith through the world. "She advanced in identical and anonymous and deliberate wagons as though through a succession of creakwheeled and limpeared avatars, like something moving forever and without progress across an urn" (p. 5), Faulkner tells us, and she thus becomes a third aspect of the urn or vase image, one neither removed and inhuman like Hightower's or horribly imperfect and repulsive like Joe's, but simply right and natural and combining both.[21] When she senses the child within her, "she sits quite still, hearing and feeling the implacable and immemorial earth, but without fear or alarm" (p. 26). At the birth of her child, Hightower observes, "More of them. Many more. That will be her life, her destiny. The good stock peopling in tranquil obedience to it the good earth; from these hearty loins without hurry or haste descending mother and daughter" (p. 384). Faulkner has recently said of her, "It was her destiny to have a husband and children, and she knew it and so she went out and attended to it without asking help from anyone. . . . She was never for one moment confused, frightened, alarmed. She did not even know that she didn't need pity" (*Paris Rev.*, p. 50). In one sense she symbolizes the basic natural order in a way very like Whitman's "placid and self-contain'd" animals in "Song of Myself."[22] But in another sense she is the "Queen Goddess of the World," whose rightness in the order of things stands in religious contrast to the Dark Temptress, the symbol and source of sin. In some form or other both always exist in religions.[23] In traditional

---

[21] Norman H. Pearson, in "Lena Grove," *Shenandoah*, III (Spring 1952), 3–7, has the provocative idea that Lena is the "leaf-fringed legend" and the "foster-child of silence and slow time" of Keat's "Ode to a Grecian Urn."

[22] The passage reads:

I think I could turn and live with animals, they're so placid and self-contain'd,
I stand and look at them long and long.
They do not sweat and whine about their condition,
They do not lie awake in the dark and weep for their sins,
They do not make me sick discussing their duty to God,
Not one is dissatisfied, not one is demented with the mania of owning things,
Not one kneels to another, nor to his kind that lived thousands of years ago,
Not one is respectable or unhappy over the whole earth.

(ll. 684–691)

[23] See Campbell, *The Hero With A Thousand Faces*, pp. 109–126, 297–302.

Christian symbolism they are the Virgin and the Whore of Babylon.

To the degree that Lena Grove symbolizes this earth-mother, Byron Bunch, the simple, good, and unthinkingly religious man, symbolizes the loving service of this natural order which the mass of mankind renders. Together they form a religious symbol of a stable order.

This elemental and eternal aspect of Lena is further enhanced by Faulkner's presenting her story and that of Byron Bunch largely in the present tense. The bulk of the stories of Joe Christmas and of Gail Hightower come to us through elaborate patterns of retrospect and character narration, so that they are in the past tense, and Faulkner is, as we have already noted, anxious to maintain a distinction between present action and antecedent action. Yet the use of the present tense for most of the Lena Grove story and for comparatively little of the other stories, gives her narrative a special quality; for the present tense is the tense of eternal truths, of continuing and forever reduplicating actions; the past tense stamps the action with tragic finality. Faulkner has recently said, "Time is a fluid condition which has no existence except in the momentary avatars of individual people. There is no such thing as *was*—only *is*" (*Paris Rev.*, p. 52). Lena belongs in the world of eternal truths, in the world of *is*.

With the birth of her son she becomes the Virgin of religion. As Malcolm Cowley notes, "The title of the novel . . . refers to Lena Grove and her baby. In the Mississippi backwoods, it is sometimes said of a pregnant woman . . . that she will be *light* in August or September." [24] "Light in August" then is another annunciation, declaring in Mississippi folk terms, "Unto us a child is born; unto us a son is given."

This serene and calm and eternally hopeful mother who comes a journey to give birth to her fatherless child in a strange place

---

[24] *Portable Faulkner*, p. 652. It has been called to my attention by several people that Faulkner is said orally to have questioned Cowley's Mississippi folklore. However, the reading here given is physically appropriate to the action of the story and to the broad meaning of the theme, whether such a folk saying does or does not in fact exist. Cottrell (*Modern Fiction Studies,* II, 213), has an excellent discussion of the complex meanings of the title: "The light is certainly two things in connection with Joanna Burden—the light in her bedroom which brings about her ruin and the subsequent blaze of her home. The same light is seen by Lena as ominous but she does not understand its full implications. . . . Lena's baby is born in the light of dawn, and the birth makes her, in the country phrase, 'light' again in the month of August. Joe Christmas' skin is light—neither black nor white . . ."

has similarities, too, to Joe's mother Milly Hines. Both are unwed; both suffer from family disapproval, although in differing degrees; both have lovers who are disreputable betrayers. But their similarity is most apparent in the children they bear. Lena's son is presented as a new Joe. When he is born, old Mrs. Hines confuses him with Joe Christmas as a baby, saying, "It's Joey.... It's my Milly's little boy" (p. 376), and she settles down grimly to protect him against Eupheus, lest he be stolen away again. The child sets into motion again what Gavin Stevens calls her "hoping machine" (p. 421). He says, "I don't think that it ever did start until that baby was born out there this morning, born right in her face, you might say; a boy too. And she had never seen the mother before, and the father at all, and that grandson whom she had never seen as a man; so to her those thirty years [since she had seen Joe] just were not" (pp. 421–422). Lena herself gets confused as to the parentage and identity of the child. She says, "She [Mrs. Hines] keeps on calling him Joey. When his name aint Joey. And she keeps on ... talking about— She is mixed up someway. And sometimes I get mixed up too, listening, having to ..." (p. 387). For Hightower the birth is a rejuvenating act. He goes home thinking, "Life comes to the old man yet ..." Usually he sleeps a great deal. "He goes to the door [of his bedroom] and looks in, with that glow of purpose and pride, thinking, 'If I were a woman, now. That's what a woman would do: go back to bed to rest.' He goes to the study. He moves like a man with a purpose now, who for twenty-five years has been doing nothing at all between the time to wake and the time to sleep again" (p. 383). Lena's child is indeed a "newer hope."

Faulkner recently commented on the "trinity" represented in *A Fable* "by the young Jewish pilot officer who said 'This is terrible. I refuse to accept it, even if I must refuse life to do so,' the old French Quartermaster General who said, 'This is terrible, but we can weep and bear it,' and the English battalion runner who said, 'This is terrible, I'm going to do something about it' " (*Paris Rev.*, p. 42–43). In one sense Hightower is like the Jewish pilot who refused life; Joe Christmas is like the Quartermaster General who could weep and bear it; and Lena's son bears the eternal hope that this one is the one who will do something about it. Thus Faulkner's threefold Christ is complete: the Christ who is "a matchless example of suffering and sacrifice and the promise of hope" (ibid., p. 42). Hightower is a symbol of suffering, however impotent and inward; Joe Christmas is a symbol of sacrifice, however private and ineffectual; and Lena's child is a symbol of hope.

This son of Lena has almost no plot relation to Joe; their links are temporal and accidental; their life lines never cross. More binds them, however, than the accident of Mrs. Hines's confusion or the similarities between their mothers. Both are the volitionless inheritors of a social stigma transmitted through their parents: in Joe's case the suspected taint of Negro blood, in the baby's case the fact of his being born out of wedlock. These facts are stigmata that isolate their bearers from their fellowmen, distinguishing them as in some sense "guilty," because of the attitudes of society; and in the puritanical and race-conscious Yoknapatawpha County in which the novel is laid they are blots that have the implication of immitigable evil. It is in order that Lena's son may not achieve the social acceptance of having a legal father that Byron Bunch must go with the mother and the young child as an unwed rather than a wed Joseph as they leave Jefferson and Mississippi. Both Joe and the child bear the social stigmata that are the outward signs of inward states. And Faulkner has so juxtaposed them that they suggest that everyman, like Joe, like Lena's son, has laid upon him the intolerable burden of human institutional coldness and inadequacy (here represented by the church and the atrophy of the religious spirit), the obligations and the abuses of the natural order (here represented by sex), and the accumulated human guilt or original sin (here represented by the bastardy and the tainted blood). And they suggest, too, that everyman is charged with rebelling against these oppressions, and that it is this rebellion, this refusal to accept which is the divine in man, the secret of his hope, the key to "a spirit capable of compassion and sacrifice and endurance," the qualities that assure that "he will prevail." [25]

The three concluding chapters, drawing together the three main strands of the story, suggest by their content and method this same threefold view. Chapter xix tells, belatedly from a narrative sense, of the death of Joe Christmas, ending as his yielding-up of the black blood in death imprisons him in the spectators' "memories forever and ever" (p. 440); thus we see Joe last in his sacrificial dying. Chapter xx shows us Hightower, whose understanding of the situations has been sharp but whose sympathy has been too frail to support action, as he views the world, himself, and his ministry honestly in the moments before he dies; thus we see him last

---

[25] Faulkner, speech accepting the Nobel Prize for Literature, quoted from *Ten Modern Masters,* ed. Robert G. Davis (New York, 1953), p. 506.

in his awareness that he has failed the church (and implicitly that the church has thus failed) because he failed in the primary human relations, that the religious spirit must express itself in service to those like Joe and Lena. In Chapter xxi Lena, Byron, and the child move toward Tennessee, and the narrative comes to us through the detached, comic report of a furniture dealer; thus the child of hope and the earth-mother are seen at last, as Lena had been at first, moving serenely and dispassionately through the world of men and seasons, remote and somehow eternal, preserved in the amber of the comic spirit.

None of these characters are in themselves alone adequate representations of the Christ story or of those elements in it which have special meaning for Faulkner; but each of them is a representation of certain limited aspects of Christ, so that we may look upon them all and the complex pattern of actions through which they move and see, as it were, the dim but discernible outline of Christ as the organizing principle behind them. Viewed in such terms as these the separate story strands are fused into a thematic whole, and it is a whole unified by Faulkner's extensive use of the Christ story and his application of a nontheological interpretation in which Christ is the suffering servant of *Isaiah,* the archetype of man struggling against the order and condition of himself and his world. In a sense he would have us look upon the impotent, suffering despair of Hightower, the "old disaster" of the sacrificially dead Joe Christmas, and the "newer hope" of Lena's son and to say of them all, with Walt Whitman:

> . . . I think this face is the face of the Christ himself,
> Dead and divine and brother of all, and here again he
>   lies.[26]

---

[26] "A Sight in Camp in the Daybreak Gray and Dim," ll. 14–15.

Robert M. Slabey

Myth and Ritual in
Light in August

After reading *A Fable* (1954), some critics were moved to re-examine the less overt Passion Week parallels in Faulkner's earlier novels. *Requiem for a Nun* (1951), however, with its combination of semiritual drama and mythic picture of the continuity and evolutionary history of human experience in the essays, did not inspire an examination of the structure of myth and ritual in Faulkner's earlier novels. And many commentators have been impressed by the mystique in "The Bear," treating its record of a religious retreat and ceremonial cleansing too often as if it were a unique or extremely rare occurrence in Faulkner's work.

By this time the Christian symbolism which accompanies the Joe Christmas story in *Light in August* has been so extensively pointed out that there is little need to repeat the details; however, nearly every attempt to explain the use of these details has failed, partially because of Faulkner's method in the novel, which is inverted, ironic, sometimes inconsistent. If Joe Christmas is to be considered in any sense as a "Christ-figure," a preliminary observation must be made: Joe embodies a "negative incarnation": i.e., he is not God humanized but man dehumanized, not God accepted as a human being but man rejected as a human being. The abundant Christian allusions emphasize the lack of love and peace in the modern world where life is based, not on love, but on force and law. Speaking in regard to *A Fable*, Faulkner has said that if Christ returned to earth, he would have to be crucified again. An earlier Faulkner character, Harry Wilbourne in *The Wild Palms*, says approximately the same thing:

> There is no place for [love] in the world today, not even in Utah. We have eliminated it. It took us a long time, but man is resourceful and limitless in inventing too, and so we have got rid of love at last

From *Texas Studies in Literature and Language*, II (Autumn, 1960), 328–349. Revised by the author. Reprinted by permission of *Texas Studies in Literature and Language* and of the author.

just as we have got rid of Christ. We have radio in the place of God's voice . . . If Jesus returned today we would have to crucify him quick in our own defense, to justify and preserve the civilization we have worked and suffered and died shrieking and cursing in rage and impotence and terror for two thousand years to create and perfect in man's own image.[1]

In this passage the point is that the world has lost the Christian view; in *Light in August* the point is that the church has lost its spiritual function. This attitude is somewhat like Kierkegaard's attack upon Christendom, a protest not against the church as an institution but against the *un*Christian situation in a presumably "Christian" society; Kierkegaard indicted the complacent code of bourgeois ethics and formalized religious practice which had replaced the Christian ideals of love and self-denial.

In *Light in August*, Christ is only a word, a curse. Not once is the Name invoked in a pious manner. The interjection is frequently on the lips of Max, is uttered by Percy Grimm before he slays Joe, and receives its ultimate degradation in the mind of Joe, when, in bed with the prostitute Bobbie, he thinks, "Jesus, Jesus. So this is it." (P. 170) Joe becomes a concrete embodiment of this profanity—through rape, perversion, robbery, sadism, murder. Doc Hines calls the name "Christmas" "a sacrilege"; McEachern calls it "heathenish." But it must be recalled that it was the nurses who named Joe; like many people, they were close to Christmas but far from Christ.

In no one of the numerous treatments of Joe as a "Christ-figure" [2] is there a truly adequate or satisfactory discussion of the complete meaning and artistic function of Joe as "Christ." It has appeared obvious to all that Faulkner was using Christian symbols and that therefore Joe must be a Christ-figure; I hope to make it evident how Faulkner is using Christian motifs and how Joe is *not* a Christ-figure. The Christian symbolism is part of a more general

---

[1] *The Wild Palms* (New York, 1939), p. 136. See Faulkner's comments in *Faulkner at Nagano,* ed. Robert A. Jelliffe (Tokyo, 1956), p. 159. All page references to *Light in August* are to the Modern Library edition (New York, 1950).

[2] Beekman W. Cottrell's article "Christian Symbols in 'Light in August'" (*Modern Fiction Studies,* II [1956], 207–213) is a fairly good accumulation of data, although his interpretation is highly questionable. C. Hugh Holman's "The Unity of Faulkner's *Light in August*" (*PMLA,* LXXIII [1958], 155–166) is an attempt to reveal "the pervasive paralleling of character traits, actions, and larger structural shapes to the story of Christ."

theme of "death-and-rebirth" which presents a hero who has many different names—and perhaps even, as Campbell says, a "thousand faces"—but who is essentially the same primordial figure. The life cycle and personal problems of Joe Christmas are less directly related to those of Christ than they are to the archetypal story of the dying god and his resurrection, which symbolized the seasonal death and reappearance of vegetation, a myth found in a large area of the world, from western Asia to the British Isles, and the subject of Frazer's *The Golden Bough.*

The mythic hero was called Tammuz in Babylon (his rites being mentioned in Ezekiel viii. 14) and Adonis (supposedly from the Semitic *adon* "lord") in Syria. His experience was closely parallel to the Phrygian Attis and the Egyptian Osiris and less directly to the Scandinavian Balder, the English John Barleycorn, and the Celtic Diarmud. There is evidence that Faulkner knew Frazer's work,[3] and it is not improbable that in *Light in August* he made use of the Adonis myth, either unconsciously or deliberately. In "The Bear" Faulkner appears to be following some of the details of the ritualistic pattern described in Frazer's discussion of "Killing the Sacred Bear." (*Golden Bough,* complete ed., VIII, 180–203) In *The Hamlet* Eula Varner, explicitly described as "Venus," in her departure from Frenchman's Bend with Flem Snopes re-enacts the goddess's seasonal absence from the world during which the earth is scorched under the sun and no living thing blooms or is born. (*Golden Bough,* abrd. ed., pp. 325–326) [4] And in *Sanctuary* there appears to be a perverted enactment of the fertility rite of the corn spirit. (*Ibid.,* pp. 399–424) Whether Faulkner used these traditional symbols "naturally" or with definite artistic purpose,

---

[3] Carvel Collins asserts that Faulkner's friends at New Orleans in the mid-twenties recall discussions of Freud, Joyce, and Frazer ("The Pairing of *The Sound and the Fury* and *As I Lay Dying," Princeton University Library Chronicle,* XVIII [1957], 123). Some basic references for the Adonis myth: Ovid, *Metamorphoses,* x, 519–739. Sir James George Frazer, *The Golden Bough: A Study in Magic and Religion,* 1 vol. abridged ed. (New York, 1922), pp. 324–356. Arnold J. Toynbee, *A Study of History* (London, 1954), VII, 412–413, 423, 457 ff., 494; X, 143.

[4] This is "The Long Summer" section of the novel, in which relief for the desiccated land from an intense and prolonged drought and an unusually harsh winter comes only upon Eula's return with her baby in the spring. Karl E. Zink identifies this as a "Persephone" likeness ("Faulkner's Garden: Woman and the Immemorial Earth," *MFS,* II [1956], 140–141). See also Carvel Collins' discussion of the Demeter-Persephone-Kore myth in *As I Lay Dying* (*Princ. U. Libr. Chron.,* XVIII, 119–123).

aware of their literary and anthropological sources (as Eliot did in *The Waste Land*) is an interesting speculation but one with which at the present I am not concerned. Whatever the case may be, the literary critic may make *post facto* use of myth as a tool in analyzing certain aspects of a novel when a particular mythic pattern can offer a cogent and illuminating explication.

There are numerous likenesses between the Adonis-myth and the story of Joe Christmas. The circumstances of conception and birth are unusual. The child (Adonis, Joe) is conceived at a secret rendezvous; when the sin of the child's mother (Myrrha, Milly) is discovered, her father (Cinyras, Doc Hines) seeks vengeance, attempting to kill both mother and unborn child. In spite of his wrath, the child is born, although his mother dies after a difficult, unaided labor. The baby is spirited away and reared by foster parents. As a man, there is a conflict between a light and a dark side. And he is killed as a result of his amorous entanglements; at the end of a chase he dies after having been castrated in a particularly horrible fashion. (The wound of Adonis is always a symbolic castration if not an anatomical one.)

The lover of Adonis is Aphrodite. In mythology there are two Aphrodites: the Uranian goddess of spiritual love and Aphrodite Pandemos, the goddess of "natural" love. The two loves are combined within the character of Joe's mistress Joanna Burden. She is consistently described as a dual personality, as "two sisters," "two creatures that struggled in the one body like two moon-gleamed shapes struggling drowning in alternate throes upon the surface of a black thick pool beneath the last moon." (P. 228) Here the two sides of Venus are perverted: spiritual love becomes a fierce asceticism ("the abject fury of the New England glacier"); earthly love becomes erotic wallowing in a sewer ("the fire of the New England biblical hell," p. 225). Joanna is two people: by day, calm, cold-faced, hard, and manlike; at night "living not alone in sin but in filth," passing through "every avatar of a woman in love." (P. 226) The morning after Joe has raped her, he is shocked by her altered appearance; he thinks *"Under her clothes she cant even be made so that it could have happened."* (P. 206) The detail of Joanna's gorgonlike features ("her wild hair, each strand of which would seem to come alive like octopus tentacles," p. 227) reveals the dark side of woman—night, evil, and sin. The numinous heads of the Gorgon and the Medusa are symbols of the devouring and the destructive; the serpents are aggressive phallic elements characterizing the fearful aspects of the goddess about whom there is a suggestion of erotic perversion.[5] Besides the snake, phallic symbols which would be associated with "the Terrible Mother" and accompany Joanna are the keys, her candle, and the monstrous old revolver "viciously poised like the arched head of a snake." (P. 247) Joanna is the twentieth-century Venus described in *The Wild Palms*—"a soiled man in a subway lavatory with a palm full of French post-cards."

Parallels with other aspects of the Adonis myth, though not always consistent, are interesting, and the cumulative effect and counter relationship of the evidence are impressive. Bobbie Allen, the short, large-handed, "immobile and down looking" waitress is a Persephone figure.[6] Her "rape" takes place in a field; as a goddess of fertility her rites involved menstrual lunar aspects; while the goddess always carried an ear of corn, Bobbie is hardly ever without something in her hand, food or a cigarette. Both Joanna and Bobbie are masculine (even in their names) and sterile, not voluptuous and fertile. Bobbie's "mother" Mame is a Demeter figure. She is described as being "violenthaired." (P. 153) The job of this goddess-madam is to initiate "newlyweds" into the secrets of marriage; protector of vegetation and proprietor of a shabby back-street restaurant, she is able to punish her enemies by condemning them either to insatiable hunger or to severe attacks of indigestion. The residence of Persephone is, of course, Hades, "the house where all the people had died," (P. 192) which appears shadowy and amorphous to Joe in his semiconscious state. While in the "Under world," the hero is the subject of a dispute: whether he (Adonis, Joe) belongs to the Dark or the Light ("under world" or "upper world," Negro or White).

Percy Grimm's pursuit of Christmas is enacted with some of the ritualistic details of the hunt (Grimm comments on Joe's clever-

---

[5] Erich Neumann, *The Origins and History of Consciousness*, trans. R. F. C. Hull (New York, 1954), pp. 87, 155; Northrop Frye, *Anatomy of Criticism* (Princeton, 1957), p. 196. Joanna, like Medusa, is decapitated. Cf. Arthur A. Miller, "An Interpretation of the Symbolism of Medusa," *The American Imago,* XV (1958), 389–399. Carvel Collins speculates about a possible source for the manner of Joanna's death in the punishment of prophets in the *Inferno,* canto xx ("Faulkner and Certain Earlier Southern Fiction," *College English,* XVI [1954], 95).

[6] Whether an intentional pun is to be found in Persephone's title "Queen of the Under World" (*quean*—"prostitute") is an interesting conjecture. The Semitic *Adonai* ("lord"), like the name *Christ,* was a title rather than a proper name. The only Faulkner character named "Jesus" is Nancy's husband in "That Evening Sun." Nancy is the "nun" ("prostitute") in *Requiem for a Nun.*

ness, "good man," and Joe thinks that "there was a rule to catch
[him] by"). Freud summarizes the fate of the Adonis figure as
"punishment through castration or through the wrath of the father
god appearing in animal form." [7] Grimm, related to the boar of
some versions of the story, here acts as the "agent" of Doc Hines's
wrath. Grimm pursues Christmas on a bicycle which he seized
from the Western Union boy who had been "leading his bicycle by
the horns like a docile cow"; (P. 402) the "horns" are phallic symbols related to the horns of the boar. In some Adonis rites the boar
is sacrificed to the god as his enemy, and in some cults Adonis is
identified with the beast that goared him: in Hightower's vision of
the wheel Grimm's face is fused with Joe's. Viewed in this light,
Grimm is the external embodiment of the inherited destructive
tendencies within Joe. The townspeople say about Joe's execution,
"It was as though he had set out and made his plans to passively
commit suicide." (P. 388) The slayer of the god in the sacred pre-
cincts (the sacred wood of Nemi) was always a young priest; in
the sanctuary of the minister's house, Grimm's voice is described
as "clear and outraged like that of a young priest." (P. 406) In
Light in August the death of the hero is accompanied not by the
usual wail of mourners but by the scream of the fire siren, mount-
ing "toward its unbelievable crescendo, passing out of the realm
of hearing."

The Keatsian imagery of the novel has been pointed out by several commentators; [8] and Joe Christmas is related to the mythological figure Shelley chose to represent Keats in his famous elegy.
Both "Adonais" and *Light in August* have in their backgrounds
cyclic movements: both heroes achieve "poetic immortality"; the
dying Christmas

> seemed to rise soaring into their [the onlookers'] memories forever
> and ever. They are not to lose it, in whatever peaceful valleys, be-
> side whatever placid and reassuring streams of old age, in the mir-
> roring faces of whatever children they will contemplate old disasters
> and newer hopes. It will be there, musing, quiet, steadfast, not fading

---

[7] Sigmund Freud, *Totem and Taboo,* in *The Basic Writings,* ed. A. A. Brill
(New York, 1938), p. 924.
[8] Richard Chase, *The American Novel and Its Tradition* (New York, 1957),
pp. 210–219; Phyllis Hirshleifer, "As Whirlwinds in the South: An Analysis
of *Light in August,*" *Perspective,* II (1949), 225–238; Alfred Kazin, "The
Stillness of 'Light in August,'" *Partisan Review,* XXIV (1957), 519–538; and
Norman Holmes Pearson, "Lena Grove," *Shenandoah,* III (1952), 3–7.

and not particularly threatful, but of itself alone serene, of itself alone triumphant. (P. 407) [9]

In this same scene, one of the most striking and memorable in modern literature, Shelley's dying meteor image (stanza 12) is reversed with Faulkner's description of the way Joe's blood rushed out "like the rush of sparks from a rising rocket"; the mechanistic images of the rocket and the meaningless wail of the siren, details of the world of harsh fact, are in awesome contrast with the placid, eternal images of Nature. In many versions of the Adonis myth, the hero is associated with a fertility goddess, who is his lover (and sometimes his mother): Tammuz with Ishtar, Adonis with Aphrodite (or Astarte), Attis with Cybele, Osiris with Isis. In *Light in August* it is Lena Grove who is pictured as a primeval earth mother; thus the dying god and loving goddess of the myth are separated—as a matter of fact they never meet—the reason being that there is no love in the world of the novel. Instead of his dead body resting in the arms of his bereaved lover, Joe's body is entrusted to the Railway Express Agency for return to the Hineses in Mottstown.

Of course Faulkner did not have to make up the Christ-Adonis parallel; it had already been suggested, in the second century by Saint Justin Martyr, and in the twentieth by Frazer, Freud, and Eliot, whose writings were known to him. Certainly, greater spiritual and moral implications appear when the Christian myth is invoked than when the pagan myth alone is utilized. (If the "theology" of this association—which has also been made by Toynbee —is distasteful to some, it must be emphasized that Faulkner *the novelist* is by no means orthodox in his treatment of Christian materials.)

To state that Faulkner was familiar with *The Golden Bough* and that certain features of the Adonis myth are present in *Light in August* is in reality to do no more than to direct the reader along the road to Xanadu; how the myth was used by

---

[9] See Jean-Paul Sartre's comments on this scene (how the sadist experiences the absolute alienation of his being from the Other's freedom), *Being and Nothingness,* trans. Hazel Barnes (New York, 1956), pp. 405–406. John Longley believes that Joe's suffering far transcends the time and the place and the means Faulkner has used, and comes to stand for everything that is grave and constant in the human condition: "Joe Christmas: The Hero in the Modern World," *Virginia Quarterly Review,* XXXIII (1957), 246.

Faulkner (or is being used by the critic) is the important aesthetic question. My purpose is not to identify immediate sources but to suggest a parallel with other works in an "eternal" pattern. Mythographers have explained the Adonis story as a vegetation myth (Frazer), a solar myth (Max Müller), a myth of sexual impotence and resurgence (Freud), or as a combination of these (Bayle).[10] In *Light in August,* each of these interpretations is to some extent possible; however, here the myth is primarily representative of a spiritual experience.

The whole novel in general (and Joe's seven-day flight after the murder in which he "travelled farther than in all the thirty years before," p. 296) is in a sense a night journey, a ritual of death and rebirth, of withdrawal and return. This is a solitary descent into the dark jungle, the depths of the sea, a strange land, the desert, the abyss—into the labyrinthine regions of the unconscious—followed by a rebirth into a new attitude or way of life, a new spiritual unity. Jung in his writings treats extensively of what he considers to be the central psychic adventure of mature human life, what he calls "the archetype of transformation" or the process of individuation and the integration of the personality. This is the same process of death of the old life and birth of the new which was traced by Frazer as the inner meaning of the fertility cults. The Cambridge critics (Murray, Cornford, Jane Harrison) have seen the ritual festivals of the vegetation spirit or "Year-Daemon" in the Attic celebrations of Dionysus as the beginnings of tragedy and comedy. Religions linked the idea of death and miraculous restoration of life with a parallel spiritual process. Toynbee applied this process to his study of the rise and fall of civilizations. The "way" of the Western mystics has been analyzed by Evelyn Underhill according to an analogous movement.[11] And a central aspect of *The Waste Land,* and a great deal of Eliot's other poetry as well,[12] is this age-old symbolic pattern, lived through as an intense per-

---

[10] Richard Chase, *Quest for Myth* (Baton Rouge, 1949), pp. 11–12.

[11] *Mysticism: A Study of the Nature and Development of Man's Spiritual Consciousness,* 17th ed. (London, 1949), pp. 167–175 *passim.*

[12] Elizabeth Drew, *T. S. Eliot: The Design of His Poetry* (New York, 1949). For discussions of withdrawal-and-return, see Joseph Campbell, *The Hero With A Thousand Faces* (New York, 1956), especially pp. 17–25, 30–40. Maude Bodkin, *Archetypal Patterns in Poetry* (New York, 1958), pp. 25–86. Arnold J. Toynbee, *A Study of History,* abridged ed. (New York, 1947), I, 217–230. P. W. Martin, *Experiment in Depth* (New York, 1955). R. W. B. Lewis identifies the design of experience, according to major American writers, as a spiritual journey from sunlight through the fires of hell to a final serenity (*The American Adam* [Chicago, 1955], p. 134).

sonal experience and accepted as the central truth of a religious faith.

The "rebirth" of Joe Christmas may be considered in three ways: (1) *physically*—Faulkner asserts the "endurance" and continuous flow of life by having Lena's baby born where Joe lived and where Joanna was murdered and on the same day that Joe and Hightower die; (2) *spiritually*—This is accomplished through a psychic withdrawal-and-return ritual; (3) *poetically*—Joe is "reborn" as an everlasting memorial in the sensibilities of those members of the community who witness his execution.

The psychological descent into the abyss and the meeting with the "shadow" of the myths are not exactly the same thing as the Existentialist's metaphysical "Encounter with Nothingness," but they are parallel to it on another level of experience. Existentialism and myth share the same general concept (it is necessary to die in order to live), the same task (to establish the self as an individual), and the same dramatic structure (a withdrawal from the external, trivial, limited, desperation-filled wasteland and a return "transfixed" and illumined by freedom and an expanded consciousness). Existentialism and myth convey a sense of life as filled with confrontations and encounters; both assert the reality and the important place in the human condition of the nonrational. Existentialism makes use of the rebirth archetype, and myths are concerned with basic problems of human existence. Joseph Campbell explains the mythic adventure in this way:

> The agony of breaking through personal limitations is the agony of spiritual growth. Art, literature, myth and cult, philosophy, and ascetic disciplines are instruments to help the individual past his limiting horizons into spheres of ever-expanding realization. As he crosses threshold after threshold, conquering dragon after dragon, the stature of the divinity that he summons to his highest wish increases, until it subsumes the cosmos. Finally, the mind breaks the bounding sphere of the cosmos to a realization transcending all experiences of form—all symbolizations, all divinities: a realization of the ineluctable void. (*The Hero,* p. 190)

"The ineluctable void" or "openness" is that "into which the mind must plunge alone and be dissolved." (*Ibid.,* p. 258) The ultimate goal of the hero is "not to *see,* but to realize that one *is* that essence; then one is free to wander as that essence in the world. Furthermore: the world too is of that essence. The essence

of oneself and the essence of the world: these two are one . . .
Thus . . . exile brings the hero to the Self in all." (*Ibid.*, p. 386)

Helmut Kuhn describes the Existentialist's Encounter with
Nothingness thus: "Nothingness is to be encountered in despair,
to be grasped in the light of anguish until, thanks to the resilience
of his self-assertive will, man emerges into the untrammeled freedom of his selfhood. He must become homeless in order to learn
about his divinity." [13] The experience of estrangement and for-
lornness is the encounter with Nothingness in the world. The first
phase of the Existentialist encounter is a descent to the nadir of
despair; this is a passage through "The Everlasting No," a crisis,
an "Extreme" or "Limit" situation, a "Shipwreck" (Jaspers); this
is the mystic's Dark Night of the Soul with its sense of dryness,
ennui, emptiness. Through the willing of despair and the facing
and acceptance of Nothingness, there is an Existentialist con-
version, an insight into Being and man's place in the world; freedom is won, responsibility for one's freedom is realized, and
authentic existence is attained. This is followed by an affirmative
phase which resembles a spiritual rebirth; this is an ascent to a
new and supposedly unassailable position—Jaspers' "elevation to
transcendence." Dorothy Norman, in her study of the correspondence between the mythological "Heroic Encounter" and life
today, comments on twentieth-century anxiety, depersonalization,
and spiritual crisis: "It is asserted that, in ages to come, our
epoch will be regarded as Existentialist in a purely negative sense,
since, at no previous time in the history of the world, have the
darkest depths of the human predicament been so piteously laid
bare." [14]

The internal conflict in Joe Christmas is basically between dark
and light—"black blood" in a "pale body"; it is reinforced symbolically by Joe's attire, "steady white shirt and pacing dark legs."
(P. 101) Gavin Stevens' rather overly logical analysis of Joe's
motives is significant because it explicitly comments on the tension
between his white blood and his black blood: "his blood would
not be quiet, let him save it. It would not be either one or the

---

[13] *Encounter with Nothingness: An Essay on Existentialism* (Chicago, 1949),
p. xv. Some of the following comments are based on Kuhn's analysis. Cf.
Faulkner's comment on Joe at the orphanage: "five is still too young to have
learned enough despair to hope" (p. 123).
[14] *The Heroic Encounter* (New York, 1958), p. 5. To explain the rhythm of
experience in Camus' works, R. W. B. Lewis, in *The Picaresque Saint* (New
York, 1959), uses a quotation from Marguerite de Navarre, sixteenth-century
"Christian humanist": *"Descender plus bas pour monter plus hautement."*

other and let his body save itself." Gavin associates the Black blood with primitivism, passion, violence, hatred, with mechanical, compulsive action, with death-seeking motives; the White with reason, peace, love, with "natural," free acts, with life-affirming motives. (Pp. 393–394) The interior struggle between two planes of being in the novel is similar to the Oriental concept of *Yin* and *Yang*. *Yin* is dark, female, night, earth, the unconscious, anonymity; *Yang* is white, male, day, heaven, consciousness, identity. The interaction of *Yin* and *Yang* is believed to underly the world of forms, and together they make manifest *Tao* ("road" or "way") which is the source and law of being.[15]

P. W. Martin explains how man to achieve self-realization must travel the way between the opposites.[16] Martin lists four sets of opposites: (1) negative versus positive; (2) the "split in the libido"—instinctual drives which man shares with animals (self-preservation, will-to-power, sexuality, etc.) versus moral and spiritual forces which oppose these drives (the dualism variously explained as body-spirit, Dionysian-Apollonian, id–super-ego); (3) the individual vs. the collective (loneliness vs. community); (4) a deep-seated but sometimes neglected opposition between time and eternity as the true setting of man's estate. To avoid psychic disorder, man must face the existence of these dualities and accept the suffering involved. The ultimate aim is a unified, authentic, fulfilled self, an integrated personality, one who has transformed his negative aspects into forces for good.

All the elements in the personality which the ego considers negative are contained in what Jung calls "the Shadow." Martin describes the Shadow as

made up of the negatives of the ego's positives. It is something which comes between a man and his fulfillment: his laziness, his feckless-ness, his tendency to let things slide or over-do things, his coward-ice, his rashness, his self-indulgence, his carping and envious nature, his murkiness and smut. In a sense the shadow is a personification of the personal unconscious, the negative expression of all those things in our life which belong to us, but which we have not been able, have not dared, to live. But it is also much more than that: the dark back-

---

[15] Campbell, *op. cit.,* p. 152.
[16] *Experiment in Depth,* pp. 139–161. Some aspects of the dualism in *Light in August* have been noted by the critics (Chase, Longley, Kazin, and Darrel Abel, "Frozen Movement in *Light in August,*" *Boston University Studies in English,* III [1957], 32–44).

ground from which we have emerged, the primitive, the animal, the non-human. (*Experiment in Depth,* p. 73)

Martin goes on to explain how a White man projects his "dark side" upon the Negro, treating him as subhuman, becoming sub-human himself when he feels it necessary to keep the "nigger" in his place. (*Ibid.*, p. 76) Eliot's "The Hollow Men" dramatizes the meeting with the Shadow, but here the poet is lost in the Shadow and his "world ends" not in any self-chosen dark night of the soul but in a sense of tormented, whimpering vacuity.[17]

After her father has told her of the doom and curse of the race, Joanna Burden comes to see Negroes as

> a shadow in which I lived, we lived, all white people, all other peo-
> ple. I thought of all the children coming forever and ever into the
> world, white, with the black shadow already falling upon them be-
> fore they drew breath. And I seemed to see the black shadow in the
> shape of a cross. And it seemed like the white babies were strug-
> gling, even before they drew breath, to escape from the shadow that
> was not only upon them but beneath them too, flung out like their
> arms were flung out, as if they were nailed to the cross. I saw all the
> little babies that would ever be in the world, the ones not yet even
> born—a long line of them with their arms spread, on the black
> crosses.

Her father tells her that she cannot escape from under the shadow:

> "You must struggle, rise. But in order to rise, you must raise the
> shadow with you. But you can never lift it to your level. I see that
> now, which I did not see until I came down here. But escape it you
> cannot. The curse of the black race is God's curse. But the curse of
> the white race is the black man who will be forever God's chosen
> own because He once cursed Him." (Pp. 221–222)

This explanation makes it clear that the inescapable curse on man, the inevitable "burden" of the human condition which man must learn to bear is "original sin," personal implication in sin and evil,

---

[17] Drew, *Eliot,* pp. 92, 97. Irene C. Edmonds, in her discussion of the Negro in Faulkner, concludes that the "Black Shadow" means two things in the fic-tion and reveals two attitudes in Faulkner: (1) the curse of slavery, and (2) the horror of miscegenation. She finds Joe to be another "tragic mulatto" stereotype ("Faulkner and The Black Shadow," in *Southern Renascence,* ed. Louis D. Rubin and Robert D. Jacobs [Baltimore, 1953], pp. 192–206).

its realization being a "Fall," a loss of innocence. Gavin Stevens believes that in Joe's hopeless attempt to escape

> there was too much running with him, stride for stride with him. Not pursuers: but himself: years, acts, deeds omitted and committed, keeping pace with him, stride for stride, breath for breath, thud for thud of the heart, using a single heart. It was not alone all those thirty years which she [Mrs. Hines] did not know, but all those successions of thirty years before that which had put that stain either on his white blood or his black blood, whichever you will, and which killed him. (P. 393)

The sex polarity in *Light in August* is most vividly detailed in three descriptions of Joe's "descent into the abyss"; each time the experience is twofold: first, the dark pit itself, followed by an awareness of its opposite, the street, thus making it possible to view their polarity in juxtaposition. Joe's first experience was at the age of fourteen with the Negro girl in the dark barn; he felt himself "enclosed by the womanshenegro"; (P. 137) leaning over her, "he seemed to look down into a black well and at the bottom saw two glints like reflection of dead stars." After the girl has fled his beating and he is engaged in fighting his comrades, there "was no She at all now ... it was as if a wind had blown among them, hard and clean." Joe's terrifying night walk through Freedman Town (the Negro section) before he murders Joanna is related first in the anti-chronology of the novel and most fully. (Pp. 99–101) He is enclosed by the cabinshapes and the women voices talking and laughing in a strange language: "It was as though he and all other manshaped life about him had beeen returned to the lightless hot wet primogenitive Female ... It might have been the original quarry, abyss itself." Fleeing the "thick black pit," he ascends, panting and his heart thudding, into the main street and "the cool hard air of white people." During Joanna's nymphomania "It was as though he had fallen into a sewer"; (P. 224) "he was at the bottom of a pit in the hot wild darkness"; (P. 235) he "began to see himself as from a distance, like a man being sucked down into a bottomless morass." What he longed for was "the street longely, savage, and cool." (Pp. 227–228) The symbolic antithesis is between the images of the pit and the images of the breeze and the street, between female and male, wet, flaccid, hot darkness and dry, rigid, cool light. Pit and breeze are archetypes of female and male respectively: the pit is the primordial womb symbol; the procreative wind and the solar phallus symbolize the creative element in the source of the wind.[18]

Joe rejects the Female on other occasions. An autoerotic assertion of his white masculinity is accomplished in a ritualistic fashion. Standing under Joanna's window he curses her "with slow and calculated obscenity," slashes the last button of his undergarment (recalling that a woman had sewed buttons on his clothes), walks naked across the yard feeling "the dew under his feet as he had never felt dew before." As he stands by the road in the thigh-tall weeds, the headlights of an approaching car shine on his body which becomes "white out of the darkness like a kodak print emerging from the liquid," and as the car passes a white woman shrieks. He spends the night in the deserted but still faintly ammoniac stable, thinking "It's because [horses] are not women. Even a mare horse is a kind of man." (Pp. 93–95)

In contrast with these experiences there is the account of Joe's arrival at Miss Burden's in the spring—an earth ritual and a return to the womb. Lying in the copse, Joe can feel "the never-sunned earth strike, slow and receptive, against him through his clothes" and is able to breathe in "the damp rich odor of the dark and fecund earth." (P. 199) Climbing through the kitchen window, he was "a shadow returning without a sound and without locomotion to the allmother of obscurity and darkness." (P. 200) His early relations with Joanna are described in similar Freudian terms: "it had been as though he were outside a house where snow was on the ground, trying to get into the house." (P. 235) Joe's homosexuality has been accepted by several critics; his hermaphroditism (and there is a tradition that Adonis was a Hermaphrodite) is fundamentally psychic and his bisexual urges are symbolic of his opposing impulses. Freudian critics have been justified in citing as evidence the magazine which Joe reads—"of that type whose covers bear *either* pictures of women in underclothes *or* pictures of men in the act of shooting one another with pistols" (P. 96, *italics* added)—but they do not note the implications of an essentially indifferent correlative statement. They also fail to

---

[18] Neumann, *Origins and History,* pp. 14, 22. A similar type of symbolism is to be found in one of Faulkner's sketches in *The Double Dealer* (January–February 1925), the monologue of the Negro longshoreman: "But, ah God, the light on the river, and the sun; and the night, the black night, in this heart . . . The stars are cold . . . The earth alone is warm . . . The cities are not my cities, but this dark is my dark, with all the old passions and fears and sorrows that my people have breathed into it."

realize the strength of the comparative in Joe's thoughts on the McEacherns: "It was the woman: that soft kindness which he believed himself doomed to be forever victim of and which he *hated worse than* he did the hard and ruthless justice of men." (P. 147, *italics* added) [19] Joe's revulsions at "womanfilth" and sex are balanced by his numerous anonymous promiscuities ("And always, sooner or later, *the street* ran through cities, through an identical and well-nigh interchangeable section of cities without remembered names, where beneath *the dark and equivocal and symbolical archways of midnight* he bedded with the women and paid them when he had the money, and when he did not have it he bedded anyway and then told them that he was a Negro"). (P. 196, *italics* added)

The symbolism of dualities has already been discussed in the explication of the dual personality of Joanna Burden, but another aspect of the motif deserves some attention—the numerous mask images. If the "Shadow" is like Mr. Hyde, a dark inner self, the Mask is like Dr. Jekyll, the bright exterior shown to the world. The mask may be a symbol of superficiality, duplicity, or sham morality; basically its function is to cover the true nature of things. Joe hides "behind the veil, the screen, of his Negro's job at the mill"; (P. 31) he empties the whiskey methodically, "his face completely cold, masklike almost." (P. 98) The dietitian's "calm mask" hides her inner "fear and fury." (P. 110) McEachern sees Joe's face as "the face of Satan, which he knew as well." (P. 178) After he has hit McEachern, Joe looks at those around him—at "faces that might have been masks." (P. 180) The men in Max's cafe have faces indistinguishable from one another, and all are masked by cigarette smoke.

Hightower's "face is at once gaunt and flabby; it is as though there were two faces." (P. 77) He had made "it appear that he had resigned his pulpit for a martyr's reasons, when at the very instant there was within him a leaping and triumphant surge of denial behind a face which had betrayed him, believing itself safe behind the lifted hymnbook, when the photographer pressed his

---

[19] Cf. p. 23: Lena *"has no mother because fatherblood hates with love and pride, but motherblood with hate loves and cohabits."* See Faulkner's poem "Hermaphroditus" in *Mosquitoes* (New York, 1927), p. 252 (reprinted in *A Green Bough* [New York, 1933], No. xxxviii). In the symbolic representation of *Yin* and *Yang* (a circle divided by a capital *S* which represents the "Way"), there is a black spot in the white half and a white spot in the black half; thus the interpresence of opposites is shown. (See Denis de Rougemont, *Man's Western Quest* [New York, 1957], p. 16.)

bulb." (P. 428) This is the expression of a Prufrockian reluctance
to meet the world directly; Hightower also finds it necessary "To
prepare a face to meet the faces" that he meets. After having been
beaten by the masked K.K.K., Hightower withdrew into his house
and "lifted the mask with voluptuous and triumphant glee." (P.
429) Hightower's father was "two separate and complete people,"
one living in "the actual world," the other "in a world where
reality did not exist"; his old Negro slave had "a face both
irascible and calm: the mask of a black tragedy between scenes."
(Pp. 415–417) Hightower's wife's face was "a mask before desire
and hatred." (P. 420) The large number of mask images in the
Hightower part of the story are appropriate because of the barrier
thrown up between him[and the world. His re-entry into life is
brief; too long "sheltered from the harsh gale of living" (P. 410)
and conditioned to his private existence, he is not able to "stand
very much reality."

In "the depths," in the "valley of the shadow," Joe finally comes
to terms with himself; he no longer flees from the dark night; he
descends into it and emerges from the woods when it is "just
dawn, daylight." (P. 293) On the morning of the day Joe dies, it is
"just dawn" when Byron calls Hightower; (P. 344) after the baby
is delivered, "It is . . . more than dawn; it is morning: already the
sun." (P. 354) In putting on the woman's shapeless "black shoes
smelling of Negro" and riding to town in the Negro wagon, Joe,
reconciled to his fate, accepts his Black blood. "It seemed to him
that he could see himself being hunted by white men at last into
the black abyss which had been waiting, trying, for thirty years
to drown him and into which now and at last he had actually
entered, bearing now upon his ankles the definite and ineradicable
gauge of its upward moving." (P. 289) Joe loses all contact with
mechanical time, no longer feels need of sleep, and ceases to be
hungry. It "seems to him now that for thirty years he has lived
inside an orderly parade of named and numbered days like fence
pickets, and that one night he went to sleep and when he waked
up he was outside of them." (Pp. 289–290) Joe accepts the complex fate of the human condition. After he has heard of Joe's
capture, Hightower thinks that

> the past week has rushed like a torrent and that the week to come,
> which will begin tomorrow, is the abyss, and that now on the brink
> of cataract the stream has raised a single blended and sonorous and
> austere cry, not for justification but as a dying salute before its own

plunge, and not to any god but to the doomed man in the barred
cell within hearing of them and of the two other churches, and in
whose crucifixion they too will raise a cross. (P. 322)

Rhetorical similarities between Conrad's *Heart of Darkness* and
Light in August have been noted by Richard Chase; he remarks
that perhaps Christmas is distantly modeled on Kurtz (*American
Novel*, p. 215), but he does not observe some more profound affinities: the light-darkness imagery, the journey and quest motif,
the theme of self-discovery, precisely the descent into the darker
side of life (in this Christmas would be both Marlow and Kurtz),
and ultimately the realization of what it means to be a man.

There is a cyclic movement in the novel—the movement of day
into night, the cosmic cycle of month and year, the birth, reproduction, and death of all things. Faulkner utilized the seasonal
cycle of the year and the temporal cycle of the day as unifying
structural devices in his mythological poem *The Marble Faun*
(1924) where the themes of change, decay, and painful rebirth
are complemented by the struggle of opposing images—fire and
ice, dancing and immobility, spring and winter, youth and age, day
and night.[20] The cyclic theme is introduced early in *Light in
August;* in the first chapter there is a description of the desolation
wreaked upon the country by Doane's mill which destroyed all the
timber within its reach "beneath the long quiet rains of autumn
and the galloping fury of vernal equinoxes." (P. 4) Byron, Joe,
Lucas, and Lena's brother work at planing mills. The felling of trees
was considered in myths to be a ritual act, and castration and tree-
felling were closely associated and were symbolically identical.
Wood is a symbol of organic, living duration as opposed to the
inorganic, dead duration of stone and the ephemeral life of
vegetation.[21]

Just as menstruation in the novel has been used as a symbol of
what is dark and unclean, Joanna's menopause is symbolic of her
sterility—physical, moral, and spiritual. Hightower, visiting Lena
and her child, thinks of Joanna—

"Poor, barren woman. To have not lived only a week longer, until
luck returned to this place. Until luck and life returned to these

---

[20] See George P. Garrett, Jr., "An Examination of the Poetry of William
Faulkner," *Princ. U. Libr. Chron.*, XVIII (1957), 125–126. See also Faulkner's use of seasonal symbolism in the story "Dry September."
[21] *Golden Bough*, pp. 109–120, 296–323; Neumann, *Origins and History,* pp.
58–59, 70, 229–230.

barren and ruined acres." It seems to him that he can see, feel, about
him the ghosts of rich fields, and of the rich fecund black life of the
quarters, the mellow shouts, the presence of fecund women, the prolific naked children in the dust before the doors; and the big house
again, noisy, loud with the treble shouts of the generations. (P. 357)

Hightower's "vision" is of life and fertility returned to the Waste
Land. Another point of difference between Joanna and Lena
should be noted: in contrast with the violent change in Joanna's
life, Lena, "unhurried and tireless as augmenting afternoon itself,"
(P. 9) travelled down the road "with the untroubled unhaste of a
change of season." (P. 46)

Joanna's nymphomania phase is described as a "dying summer";
it began in September and, after the ebb and flow of her passion,
ended in September two years later with "the dawning of half
death." Her first phase—"it had been as though [Joe] were outside a house where snow was on the ground, trying to get into the
house"—began shortly after Joe's arrival in the spring and lasted
until fall of that year; her final phase—Joe "was in the middle of
a plain where there was no house, not even snow, not even wind"
(Pp. 235–236)—began in Joe's third September and ended the
following August; she asked Joe to go to the Negro school in the
early spring of this final year. Some of the implications of the title
Light in August are made clear in the imagery which accompanies
the narrative of the affair: "It was summer becoming fall, with
already, like shadows before a westering sun, the chill and implacable import of autumn cast ahead upon summer; something
of dying summer spurting again like a dying coal, in the fall." (P.
228) The same type of symbolism appears in the atmosphere of
Hightower's final revery—"the lambent suspension of August into
which night is about to fully come." (P. 430) Both Joanna and
Hightower are "autumn" figures and both were born into the
"autumn" of their parents' lives.

The seasonal and solar background of the novel is not in keeping with the celebration of the Christian myth in the spring, the
season of rebirth and promise. The time for the observance of the
ritual of Adonis, with its close relationship to fertility and vegetation myths, in several places (e.g., Alexandria) was in late summer,
the season of fulfillment and ripeness, with the crops ready for
harvesting, the violent destruction of vegetation by man; (*Golden
Bough*, p. 338) the "Waste Land" imagery of the novel suggests
the aridity and imminent decay and decline of an "August" world.

Most of the important events occur in the late summer or early autumn, the season of *Kathodos* (down-going); Joe's street is described as running "through yellow wheat fields waving beneath the fierce yellow days of labor and hard sleep in haystacks beneath the cold mad moon of September, and the brittle stars." (Pp. 195–196)

The novel begins and ends with a similar picture; at the end we have come full circle as it were and Lena is again on the road. There is an identification suggested between her nameless, fatherless child and Joe Christmas, who was lynched on the baby's birthday. Lena herself is even a bit confused about the paternity and identity of her child; and although she is too dull to realize the implications of the situation, the sensitive reader can. Perhaps it is not ridiculous or sacrilegious to suggest that Byron, Lena, and her baby at the conclusion of the novel—not in the specific aspects of their humble stupidity but in the broad outlines and even mythic and ritualistic character of their journey—suggest the Holy Family leaving Bethlehem; thus *on one level of symbolism* there is a suggestion of the simultaneity of Crucifixion and Nativity.[22] This concept of birth and death, creative and destructive forces existing at the same moment of Christian history is implicit in Eliot's "Journey of the Magi" and explicit in Dylan Thomas' image of the unbegotten Jesus who had already suffered on the cross.[23] In *Light in August* there may be a Nativity and a Good Friday, but there is no Easter Sunday. Some critics have suggested that Faulkner's early novels represent the world between the Fall and the Redemption; however, it is not a pre-Christian, Jewish world looking towards the Messiah, but an a-Christian world which has turned its back on the Redemption. The atmosphere is similar to that of Holy Saturday (which is Benjy Compson's birthday); Christ has been crucified, but if He has risen from the dead, the people have not heard—or have not listened to—the "good news" of his Resurrection.

In *Light in August* life is viewed as a cycle of ritualistic repetition. Joe's killing the sheep (Pp. 160–162) is a *rite de passage* (a rite of transition which ushers an individual into a new way of life or a new status)—here like a ritual initiation to puberty, an advance to new knowledge of existence. For Joe, however, it is not

---

[22] Cottrell makes a similar observation, adding that Lucas Burch as Judas is responsible for both Nativity and Crucifixion (*MFS*, II, 212).

[23] See Jacob Korg, "Imagery and Universe in Dylan Thomas' '18 Poems,'" *Accent*, XVII (1957), 3–15.

an advance to a new stage of development in masculinity, leaving
the attitudes and emotions of the previous stage, but a denial of
the existence, and an immunization against an unpleasant fact of
life, by blood cleansing blood; thus Joe struggles *against* growth
and in another way removes himself from the common inheritance
of man. Joe's execution, already discussed as a fertility rite, is also
a purification ritual, the expulsion of sins and evils from the community, the execution of one who is "tainted" or unclean, here according to racial discrimination.

The occasional wheel images in the novel are in themselves only
of passing interest, but as a part of a major pattern of symbolism
they are significant. Joanna Burden's house is described as the
hub of a wheel: Negro women "came to the house from both directions up and down the road, following paths which had been years
in the wearing and which radiated from the house like wheel-
spokes." (P. 225) It is the center of the action of the novel, the
axis mundi or the mythological "world navel," the place of death
and of birth, around which the world revolves in time and space.
The destruction of the old house in the flames is like a solemn
cleansing ceremony; everything of the old order must be removed
in preparation for the new. Toynbee, in his cyclic theory of history,
has used the metaphor of the wheel to explain the successive rises
and falls of civilizations, a rhythm in which successive revolutions
of a wheel carry a vehicle, not on the repetitive circular course that
the revolving wheel itself describes, but in a progressive movement
towards a goal.[24] The wheel-symbol in *Light in August* does not
represent monotonous, purposeless repetition (as it does, for instance, in *The Waste Land*, 1. 50) but progress towards a goal,
even if the goal is difficult to attain.

In Hightower's vision of the wheel (Pp. 427–432) it is possible
to identify the wheel as "standing for" and thinking; and, along
parallel lines, the sand as reality, the axle and the vehicle as
"knowing" or consciousness and Being or "life" respectively. At
first the wheel of thinking is described as beginning to run in sand;
Hightower sees himself surrounded by faces, "mirrors in which he
watches himself," and sees himself as he really was. Rebuked by
"the final and supreme Face Itself," he realizes that for fifty years
he has been "a single instant of darkness in which a horse galloped
and a gun crashed." Then the wheel rushes on, "freed now of burden, of vehicle, axle, all." A halo of faces appears, "peaceful, as

---

[24] *A Study of History* (London, 1954), VII, 423.

though they have escaped into an apotheosis . . . composite[s] of all the faces which he has ever seen"—Joe, Lena, and her child, the people of the town. Darrel Abel calls Hightower's vision "the serene moment of Apollonian vision in the Dionysian dance of life." [25] Hightower apparently dies, and "With this last left of honor and pride and life," the cavalry rush past and night finally comes.

Hightower's wheel is related to the ancient Mandala symbol which has appeared everywhere and in every age. The oldest form is the sun-wheel; and the mandala is also found in other rounded forms and fourfold things and such symbols as the tree of life, the cross, flower, fire.[26] Jung has interpreted it as symbolic of a psychic, inner experience and has recorded dreams in which the symbol appeared; though incomprehensible to the patient, it was accompanied by a strong feeling of harmony and peace. Its linear form is the never-ending line expressive of eternity or continuity; the most elaborate symbolism is to be found in India where life is seen as a wheel, the cosmos created and maintained by a balance of opposing forces—male and female, day and night, good and evil. Frequently associated with the mandala in religious art are the figures of the Mother and God-Child—e.g., an old Babylonian representation of the mother goddess holding the infant Tammuz and a later Christian sun-wheel of Virgin and Child. Jung concluded that Eastern and medieval mandalas emphasize the importance of the central figure, while the center of modern ones is empty, the place of the deity seemingly taken by the wholeness of man. He also found that the experience which was ultimately formulated in the mandala pattern was typical of people who were no longer able to project the divine image; the circle seemed to act like a protective enclosure, preventing any outburst and a disintegration, and protecting an inward purpose. Hightower's wheel comes close to articulating Joe's felt realization of his common humanity: "Each man is responsible for everything before everyone." Other mandala figures in *Light in August* would be the wagon-wheel image associated with Lena, and Joe's final haven behind the overturned table in Hightower's kitchen.

---

[25] *BUSE,* III, 43.
[26] See C. G. Jung, Commentary on *The Secret of the Golden Flower* (London, 1931); Frieda Fordham, *An Introduction to Jung's Psychology* (London, 1956), pp. 65–69; and Dorothy Donnelly, *The Bone and the Star* (New York, 1944), pp. 62–65, 112–117, 192–194. See also Carvel Collins' speculations concerning the possible mandala symbol in "The Bear" (*Faulkner Studies,* II [1954], 58–60).

Joe Christmas is not a "Christ" figure but a *Golden Bough* figure. The events of his life story and the imagery with which they are told are related to an archetypal experience. *Light in August* is part of an "eternal" framework: the journey of the classical hero in his mythological descent into the abyss and meeting with the Shadow (the Shadow which is his own "dark" side); the similar pattern in the modern existential encounter with Nothingness; the timeless sequence of withdrawal and return, death and rebirth, analogous to the principle of organic growth, a rhythmic experience close to the heart of Man, recorded in art and literature from prehistoric time to "atomic" time. Myths present fundamental attitudes about fundamental matters.

The final chapter of *Light in August* (the nameless furniture dealer's story of Lena and Byron) is a radical change of mood from sadness and horror to joy and humor, similar to the *peripeteia* or outburst of joy in the satyr play following the *anagnorisis* (discovery of the slain and mutilated hero) at the conclusion of the Greek tragic trilogy—which itself was parallel to the "Eniautos" celebrations of the death and rebirth of Year Spirits.[27] Thus the concluding impression in the novel is of serenity and order. Just as a balance is achieved in the healthy mind between the death instinct and the tendency towards self-preservation, there is here an affirmation that the two sides of life—sorrow and joy, dark and light, motion and stasis, flux and permanence, despair and hope— are seemingly ever in balance on the cosmic scale. The unceasing movement of the wheel suggests an unending process checking and balancing destruction with creation, death with birth, foolishness with wisdom, waste land with fertile land. In contrast with Joe Christmas's "lynching," an image of "all human misery under the sun," there is Lena, the enduring life force, pure physical well-being. There are chaos and disorder, but there are also inner peace, harmony, and stability. Lena is the Alpha and Omega of the novel (or in the words of a favorite Faulkner character "de first" and "de last"), but in terms of the vision of life presented therein she is seemingly without beginning or end; she just exists as an eternal *is*.

---

[27] Gilbert Murray, "Excursus on the Ritual Forms Preserved in Greek Tragedy," in Jane E. Harrison, *Themis* (Cambridge, 1927), pp. 343–344. The satyr play-likeness of the furniture dealer's narrative has already been suggested by Longley (*VQR*, XXXIII, 249). Irving Howe thinks that the structure of the book "resembles an early Renaissance painting—in the foreground a bleeding martyr, far to the rear a scene of bucolic peacefulness, with women working in the fields" (*William Faulkner: A Critical Study* [New York, 1952], p. 49).

Several comments by Joseph Campbell, in his discussion of the function of mythology in bridging the gap between tragedy and comedy, can illumine Faulkner's purposive juxtaposition of plot elements and his structural arrangement of parts in *Light in August:*

> The happy ending of the fairy tale, the myth, and the divine comedy of the soul, is to be read, not as a contradiction, but as a transcendence of the universal tragedy of man ... Where formerly life and death contended, now enduring being is made manifest—as indifferent to the accidents of time as water boiling in a pot is to the destiny of a bubble, or as the cosmos to the appearance and disappearance of a galaxy of stars. Tragedy is the shattering of the forms and of our attachment to the forms; comedy, the wild and careless, inexhaustible joy of life invincible. Thus the two are the terms of a single mythological theme and experience which includes them both and which they bound: the down-going and the up-coming (*kathodos* and *anodos*), which together constitute the totality of the revelation that is life, and which the individual must know and love if he is to be purged (*katharsis* = *purgatorio*) of the contagion of sin (disobedience to the divine will) and death (identification with the mortal form). (*The Hero,* p. 28)

> The dreadful mutilations are then seen as shadows, only, of an immanent, imperishable eternity; time yields to glory; and the world sings with the prodigious, angelic, but perhaps finally monotonous, siren music of the spheres. (*Ibid.,* pp. 29–30)

> [Thus] the world is [revealed as] a majestic harmony of forms pouring into being, exploding, and dissolving. But what the swiftly passing creatures experience is a terrible cacaphony of battle cries and pain. The myths do not deny this agony (the crucifixion); they reveal within, behind, and around it essential peace (the heavenly rose). (*Ibid.,* p. 288)

The interrelationship of life and death is not seen by the people of Jefferson; they fail to understand the rhythm of life and are separated from nature by the triviality and superficiality of their everyday existence.

To criticize the lack of sophistication in the use of Lena's endurance as a point of affirmation is to mistake the ineffability of its permanence and innocence, to judge it according to an alien metaphysics; this kind of resolution is justified artistically by its structural position and thematically by its mythic context. Lena, involved in but somehow above and unmoved by birth and death, represents a primordial image and ancient and lasting truths about

existence, perhaps more Oriental than Western—life as a rhythmic
cycle of births and rebirths and "the Peace that passeth understanding." And thus *Light in August*, like *The Waste Land*, concludes on a note of quiescence and hope; but unlike Eliot's poem
the conclusion here is not an abstract idea (Shantih shantih shantih) but a concrete personification of tranquility, the eternal re-
newal of life, and the triumph of the "pure in heart."

The form of *Light in August* is both tragic and comic: the content both existential and mythic; the final effect both meaningful
and affirmative. Joe Christmas faces the problem of twentieth-
century man—trying to be human in a chaotic and hostile world.
His story follows a basic pattern of experience that is found in myth,
religion, philosophy, tragic drama, and life. His discovery of himself
as a human being becomes an affirmation of the nature of man. And
love and death, birth and rebirth are revealed as part of the larger
dynamic process of life, "the eternal joy of existence." [28]

---

[28] Friedrich Nietzsche, *The Birth of Tragedy,* in *The Philosophy of Nietzsche*
(New York, 1927), p. 1039. My article "Joe Christmas, Faulkner's Marginal
Man," *Phylon*, XXI (Fall, 1960), 266–277, complements the present study.

John L. Kimmey

The Good Earth in
Light in August

Sometimes the interpretation of a novel instead of involving the
reader in the life of the book removes him from it by burying the
story beneath layer after layer of abstraction. He finds himself
thinking not of character but of symbols, not of action but of the
narrative method and prose texture, not of the meaning but of the
sociological or religious overtones. While this type of discussion is

---

From *Mississippi Quarterly,* XVII (Winter, 1963–1964), 1–8. Reprinted by
permission of *Mississippi Quarterly* and of the author.

legitimate and does tend somewhat to enrich the understanding of the work, in the main it separates the reader from his experience. He has a hard time seeing not only what he has read but also what the author intended him to read.

Light in August, in my opinion, has become the victim of a critical abstraction: namely, the Christ story.[1] Admittedly there are suggestions here and there of such a story, but on the whole they are tangential and detract from the primary concern of the novel, which is man's relationship with the natural world, one of William Faulkner's fundamental themes. Protestantism in the South, miscegenation, man's search for identity are ancillary to this basic concept that the author dramatizes on page after page in inescapable terms. To overlook it is to mistake the shadow for the substance.

At the very beginning of the novel the theme of man's relationship with the natural world is presented in two contrasting scenes. On the one hand, there is the description of the mill where Lena Grove's brother works, a mechanical monster bent on destroying all the pine trees in the area and leaving the countryside in "peaceful desolation" unfit for cultivation. When the timber has been cut, the men and machines will move on to ruin the wilderness elsewhere, abandoning the expendable machinery to rust away amid weeds and stumps. Waste and sterility are the results of this relentless exploitation of virgin forests. Nothing is permanent in such a world, nothing is meaningful, no one has any roots. The woods serve only one purpose, the greed of men.

Set against this picture is the figure of Lena Grove walking the dusty roads of Alabama and Mississippi in harmony with nature, obedient to the rhythms of the earth. She is neither afraid nor alarmed although she is unmarried and pregnant and searching for the father of her child. Around her floats the "hot still pinewiney silence of the August afternoon" (p. 7); [2] before her stretches "the sunny loneliness of the enormous land" (p. 24). Fruitfulness, purposefulness, a steady implacable movement through day to dark and dark to day govern her life. Though alone and homeless she is neither lonesome nor rootless. Though from Doane's Mill she is not a part of it. She has a faith in the "immemorial earth" that the

---

[1] Although there are many articles expressing this point of view, the best one is by C. Hugh Holman, "The Unity of Faulkner's *Light in August*," *PMLA*, LXIII (March, 1958), 155–166.

[2] *Light in August* (Modern Library, 1950). All references are to this edition of the novel.

other characters whose path she crosses either reject or are desperately seeking. As Faulkner has said of her in commenting on the book, she has "that pagan quality of being able to assume everything." [3]

Lucas Burch, the father of her unborn child, true to his rootless, rapacious character is one of the rejecters of nature. He has no feeling for the earth he tramps and destroys. Shiftless, parasitical, bumptious, he is compared to a car going along the street with the radio on and no one inside, that is, a mechanical shell of a man, as well as a locust feeding off the country. His whole character reflects the atmosphere of the mill. And when we last see him after he escapes from the deputy by slipping out the window of Lena's cabin like a long snake, he is coming out of the woods onto the railroad tracks, a fact symbolical itself of his abandonment of nature and his essential homelessness. He is compared to a trapped animal running away and hating the very earth he runs on and the air he breathes. After he beats up Byron Bunch and hops the freight to be "sucked into a vacuum," he passes his antagonist beside the tracks, a "lean, harried, desperate" face in contrast to the "mild, nondescript, bloody one" (p. 386) of Bunch gazing at him and the train in childish astonishment. And so once more we see the mill-Grove contrast whose shadows lengthen as the story develops.

Byron Bunch has the same sort of unconscious feeling for nature Lena does and moves through it as slowly and quietly as she but without her unflagging steadiness and faith. He wavers. He broods. He has to struggle both with himself and with the alien forces that Burch represents. In the scene where he is hiding in the hills watching Lena's cabin and waiting for the deputy and Burch to appear, he thinks of having to endure the loss of Lena to the father of her child. Yet he is not in despair. He knows "the two inescapable horizons of the implacable earth" (p. 372) which he must remain within forever and is not afraid. He accepts his insignificant place in the scheme of things and is not discouraged. Around him everything is peaceful and familiar, the hills, the trees, the ruined plantation in the land below. Though not quite at home in this world of natural things, he learns to come to terms with them. Though not-a courageous man he learns to keep going against great odds. While walking to Jefferson after his fight with Burch,

---

[3] *Faulkner in the University,* ed. by Frederick L. Gwynn and Joseph L. Blotner (The University of Virginia Press, 1959), p. 199.

he tries to persuade himself to go see Lena and declare his love for her, but he cannot. "He does not give up, however" (p. 387). Nor does he give up at the end of the book during the journey with Lena in the furniture dealer's truck. After leaving her one night in shame because he had surprised her indiscreetly in the truck, he returns the next day to continue his life with her, saying, "I done come too far now . . . I be dog if I'm going to quit now" (p. 443). His determination, his gritty stubbornness are what bind him to Lena and connect him with the earth.

Like Lucas Burch, Joanna Burden is alienated from nature. Her sterility, her loneliness in a land foreign to her beliefs and her blood, her sexual perversion are evidence of this fact, though unlike Burch's case it is not her fault. She does not turn on the natural world, spit at it, despise it, as he does when he finds himself trapped by it. Instead of an enemy chasing her, it is a force, a presence constantly threatening her with betrayal. She is kept awake at night by "something out of the darkness, the earth, the dying summer itself" (p. 231). And this "something" is the longing for a child. Her virginity too long has crucified her. She desires to be a part of the world to which Lena so instinctively and confidently belongs. For instance, in December she announces to Christmas, whom she has taken as a lover, that she is going to have a child, although she starts talking about the fact loosely in September to prepare him (p. 232). And the symbolism of the late summer is significant, for it is both a time of harvest and the coming of fall, of her latent fruitfulness and the approach of old age. The "shadow of autumn was upon her" (p. 230). Before she dies she wants a deeper and more basic satisfaction and fulfillment than all her passionate work on behalf of the Negroes has given her. More than a foreigner in the South, an outcast among her own race, she is a betrayer of her own womanly nature, which is equated throughout the book with the earth. When she realizes that she is not pregnant, she returns to the old sexless and monotonous life of prayer inherited from her New England ancestors, once more estranged from herself though now reunited with her grandfather and brother, who were killed for their defense of the Negroes after the Civil War. Her life again becomes one of denial and damnation. Doomed by forces beyond her control, she has no choice but to repudiate the earth she once yearned so desperately to be in accord with. Her murder stands in direct contrast to the birth of Lena's baby just as it parallels that of Joe Christmas.

Christmas, like Joanna Burden, is a stranger to the earth by

accident of birth rather than by choice. And like her he is cursed
both by the Negro problem and a harsh Calvinistic creed that are
undermining his sense of belonging to the world of men and nature.
And as in the case of the New England spinster (whose life has
been influenced by her grandfather and father) it is two men who
distort his vision of life. His grandfather Eupheus Hines instills in
him the idea he is part Negro, hence unnatural and unwanted.
McEachern hammers the harsh Presbyterian catechism into his
body and soul. (It should not be forgotten that Miss Burden's
grandfather once said, "I'll learn you to hate two things...hell
and slaveholders" [p. 212].) But there is a fundamental difference
too. On McEachern's farm Christmas, unlike Miss Burden, develops a sense of the richness and rightness of the earth without actually thinking about the process. His experiences are almost unconscious as on that Sunday he goes without food all day because of
his refusal to learn the catechism. As he lies in his room, an eight-
year old boy sulking away, moths whirl about the lamp and "from
beyond the window he could smell, feel, darkness, spring, the
earth" (p. 136), the natural world the church has driven him from.

Throughout Faulkner's account of Christmas' childhood and
adolescence on the farm there is a clear contrast between the alien
religious dogma of McEachern and the warmth and sometimes the
indifference of the earth. After his fight with the boys in the sawmill because of his vicious treatment of a Negro girl, he goes home
battered and confused, stopping at the fence and absorbing all the
various smells and sounds of the summer night. Years later when
the waitress Bobbie Allen tells him the nature of her sickness, an
account which recalls his discussion with a group of boys about
menstruation and his killing of a sheep and plunging his hands in
the blood as a result of this conversation, he flees down the road
and into the woods. However, instead of the fertility of the earth
waiting for him this time, there are the "hard trunks... hardfeel-
ing, hardsmelling..." (p. 165). He vomits. He has lost the communion with nature which he once had as a small boy and which
he does not recover for a long time.

Some fifteen years later when he comes to Joanna Burden's
house and lies in the shrubbery watching it, his feeling for the
warmth of the natural world returns. Stretched out on the ground,
he is aware of the "damp rich odor of the dark and fecund earth"
(p. 199) once more. And this sense does not leave him during his
whole stay at the house. The night he decides he must murder
Miss Burden after she has prayed over him for the last time, he

goes once more to those bushes he had lain in three years ago and hears again the myriad sounds of the night and feels again "the fecund earth" (p. 246) he first experienced on McEachern's farm. It is an earth which Faulkner constantly identifies with the "lightless hot wet primogenitive Female" (p. 100) and which Christmas is alternately fleeing from and going toward, searching for his place in the world.

His flight after the murder of Miss Burden takes him, as it took Burch, his partner, to the woods. And Faulkner observes, "It is as though he desires to see his native earth in all its phases for the first or the last time" (p. 295). Although he had been brought up in the country, he had never known anything about its "actual shape and feel." He had merely absorbed it through his pores. And even now after a week of skulking around in the secret places of nature, he remains "a foreigner to the very immutable laws which earth must obey" (p. 295). Day and dark are not, as they are to Lena during her sojourn across the face of the earth, "peaceful and undeviating changes" but meaningless shutter clicks. Yet gradually he gropes through to some kind of partial understanding of what the natural world means and what his place in it really is. Everything suddenly seems very quiet and peaceful to him. He is no longer in any haste to escape from his pursuers. Upon reaching a road, he heads for the nearest town to give himself up, as much in surrender to the earth as to the law. The "black tide" (p. 297) that creeps up his legs, evoking death, as he rides into Mottstown stems not only from the Negro boy beside him in the wagon but also from the "dark and fecund earth" that he has known throughout his whole tragic life. It finally claims him for its own. Yet when it dooms him in Hightower's kitchen and that "black tide" pours out of his castrated body, it does so serenely, triumphantly. He accepts his fate.

Hightower's attitude toward the natural world is a kind of summary of the attitude of the major characters in the book. He hates it, he fears it, he flees it. Yet he longs for the communion with it he once knew in his youth. Sitting in his house alone after a quarrel with Bunch in which he advised him to give up his love for Lena, he thinks how wonderful it would be to be young again. He hears the ceaseless murmur of the insects around the lamp. He smells, as Christmas often does, "the hot still rich maculate smell of the earth" (p. 278). Years ago how he "had loved darkness . . . sitting alone among trees at night" (p. 278). However, later on in life those trees and the earth become for him, as they did for

Christmas, "savage, filled with, evocative of, strange and baleful half delights and half terrors" (p. 278). He grows afraid of nature just as Christmas grows afraid of the natural world with respect to women. Finally like Burch he learns to hate it. And like Joanna Burden he flees to "walls, to artificial light" (p. 278). His books, especially the poems of Tennyson, become what Joanna Burden's work on behalf of the Negro becomes for her, a substitute for experience. For him, as it might be said of her, "soon the fine galloping language, the gutless swooning full of sapless trees and dehydrated lusts begins to swim smooth and swift and peaceful" (p. 278). Both of them are alone, shut in from the world, living sterile lives.

However, Hightower has one thing left to him despite his failures, and that is the image of his grandfather's death and the Confederate cavalry, which floats before him periodically at dusk. Despite the fact that his grandfather was shot while raiding a henhouse, he acted courageously, he died heroically. There was "honor and pride and life" (p. 431) in his career as a soldier that are lacking in the life of his grandson who is responsible for his own wife's suicide, who has deserted his church, who lives like a vegetable. But still Hightower aims to win for himself that "honor and pride and life." And what aids him in achieving this goal is Christmas and Lena, Christmas whom he tried to help by providing him with an alibi when the escaped prisoner darts into his house and Lena whom he assists in the birth of her baby.

It is Lena he turns to first. The assistance he gives her revives him as nothing has done in years, jerks him out of the flabby state of mind in which he has been wallowing. When he leaves the cabin at dawn after the birth, he steps down "to the earth" and walks back home thinking, "Life comes to the old man yet . . ." (p. 355). He experiences that feeling of "triumph and pride" he had only known before vicariously through the memory of his grandfather. To him Lena is one of the "good stock peopling in tranquil obedience to it the good earth" (p. 356). Upon his return to the cabin he walks through the woods Christmas used to pass through, and the scenery stimulates him. For during his walk he senses once more as he had in his youth, as Christmas had done in his youth, "the fecund odor of the earth, the woods" (p. 356). And he wonders how he ever abandoned this practice of keeping in touch with nature. It reminds him of another practice he had given up, prayer. Then suddenly the two seem to him the same. His religion is basically tied to the land, inseparable from his feeling for and belief in the land of his people with its tranquility, its acceptance of life, its forgiveness. His faith is not something that has to do with the church, the seminary, theology. It is part of Lena's "good earth."

Emerging from the woods, he contemplates the cabin where Lena is staying and the remains of the burned Burden house. He pities the murdered woman just as he pities everyone throughout the novel, Christmas, Lena, Bunch, himself. But before going in to visit the new mother he has a vision, not of the cavalry this time, but of the "ghosts of rich fields" around him, of "the rich fecund black life of the quarters, the mellow shouts, the presence of fecund women, the prolific naked children ... the big house again noisy, loud with the treble shouts of the generations" (p. 357). It is the munificent vision of the peaceful plantation, of the vigorous and hopeful life, of the good earth to which he and Joanna Burden herself had been strangers most of their lives. And it is this vision which brings Hightower out of his dead life and restores him to humanity for the time being, whereas the other vision, that of his grandfather, had acted only to confirm him in his loneliness.

The last time, however, that he sees this heroic vision while sitting in his house at dusk a change takes place in him. It is after Christmas' death and Hightower is reviewing his life, his cruelty to his wife, his hypocrisy as a preacher, the professional church set against truth and peace which he served. Suddenly in the midst of this self-laceration all the faces that had once been part of his life appear in a halo of vivid lambency. Of them all the one that stands out is that of Christmas, and blended with it to seem almost one is that of Percy Grimm. The whole scene of the murder and the castration in the kitchen materializes before the old man. And he sees in the great tragedy of Christmas (his loneliness among "the cold and terrible stars" [p. 431], his murder of Joanna Burden, his alienation from the earth) his own tragedy for the first time. It is his salvation. He does not destroy himself despite the sins he has committed, because as Faulkner says in a commentary on the book "he still tried to be a man of God ... He had to endure, to live." [4] He survives precisely because of what he has done for Lena and what he has seen of Christmas. When the cavalry thunder into his life for the last time "borne upon a cloud of dust" (p. 431), they ride not out of Tennyson but out of *Henry IV* (the play he read upon coming from the birth of Lena's baby), not out of the stagnant isolation of his middle age but out of the wild

---

[4] *Ibid.,* p. 75.

affirmation of his youth. He at last knows something of that "honor and pride and life" his grandfather experienced. Even when they cease and night has come "he still hears them." And it is this sense of triumph which keeps him in touch with the earth despite his tendency "to feel himself losing contact" with it as he envisages his grandfather.

In addition to involving his characters with the natural world, Faulkner holds his theme of man's relationship with the good earth before the reader by reference to the season and the light mentioned in the title of the novel. "It was summer becoming fall, with already, like shadows before a westering sun, the chill and implacable import of autumn cast ahead upon summer" (p. 228). Such an indefinite time between summer and fall with its shadows and chill is analogous to the indefinite time of day between afternoon and night during which most of the action takes place. Almost every scene Hightower and Christmas are in is set at dusk. And the dominant light shaping their thoughts and actions is chiaroscuro, a concept mentioned several times in the novel in regard to each character. Christmas in particular is described in terms of light and shade, white and black, as in the following passage: ". . . maple leaves sliding like scraps of black velvet across his white shirt" (p. 99). He always wears a white shirt and black trousers. Even his flight after the murder is depicted in such terms: "Time, the spaces of light and dark, had long since lost orderliness" (p. 291). Of course, this type of symbolism heightens the tension of his tragic life in which he never finds out to which race he belongs. And it is also used effectively in Joanna Burden's account of her life: "I thought of all the children coming forever and ever into the world, white, with the black shadow already falling upon them before they drew breath" (p. 221). In a similar way the copper light and the gray twilight are proper for the introspection of Hightower. He sits at his study window, "the room still dark behind him. The street lamp at the corner flickers and glares, so that the bitten shadows of the unwinded maples seem to toss faintly upon the August darkness" (p. 65). He lives between light that is going and the dark that is coming, suspended between the failure of his own life and the triumph of his grandfather, powerless to act.

Both men are aware of the night shadows and the autumn chill falling upon them in contrast to the sunny abundance of Lena. And it is this contrast and the mingling of these lights and the seasons they reflect that give a significance to the lives of Christmas, Hightower, and Lena Grove which goes beyond the Christ story. Instead, this is a story of man's relationship with the "immemorial earth" that has been going on since the first ages of man. For as Faulkner has remarked, the title of the book refers to a light evocative of a time "older than our Christian Civilization." [5]

---

[5] *Ibid.,* p. 199.

John Lewis Longley, Jr.

Joe Christmas: The Hero in the Modern World

—Aristotle has not defined pity and terror—said Stephen Dedalus—I have. Pity is the feeling which arrests the mind in the presence of whatsoever is grave and constant in human sufferings and unites it with the human sufferer. Terror is the feeling which arrests the mind in the presence of whatsoever is grave and constant in human sufferings and unites it with the secret cause.—

It is appropriate that Joyce's Stephen Dedalus should formulate this definition, for, different as he is from Joe Christmas, they are alike in being heroes who are distinctly modern and who must make their way in a cosmos that is violent, chaotic, and absurd. Stephen's plight is only slightly less desperate than Christmas', and Stephen's motto *non serviam* is very close to Christmas' rigid determination not to submit to those forces that compulsively attempt to shape him to their will.

Sutpen and John Sartoris, especially when viewed in their dynastic patterns, are tragic heroes in the grand and completely tragic mold, partly because, of course, they are located in a remote and more "heroic" time, when presumably there existed that scope of action and choice large enough for heroic gestures.

From *The Tragic Mask: A Study of Faulkner's Heroes* (Chapel Hill: The University of North Carolina Press, 1963), pp. 192–205. Reprinted by permission of The University of North Carolina Press.

But even assuming Faulkner's possession of a tragic sensibility and granting him the ability to shape it into art, how can the very long jump to Joe Christmas as tragic hero be made? There are perhaps two possible approaches to this question, and perhaps both of them should be used: to what extent is Christmas authentically tragic by traditional criteria, and to what extent can it be shown that he is tragic by some entirely modern, different set of criteria? To oversimplify vastly, the modern protagonist should be one who is typical of the age and not so remote from typical human beings as to make emotional identification difficult for the spectator. In some highly symbolic fashion, the modern hero must typify the major myths and major problems of our century. In a cosmos where all is chaos and all standards have disappeared, he will very likely be destroyed as a result of his failure to define himself correctly in relation to that cosmos. Lastly, he must somehow embody the perpetual human constants which are the property of any age. Bypassing for a moment this very interesting second possibility, let us examine Christmas in the light of traditional, classic tragic criteria. At first glance, this procedure appears unpromising.

Granting his acts of persistence, his arrogance and pride, how can Christmas be called noble? How can he be said to be illustrious in rank and fortune? Above all, how can a human being so conditioned, so utterly predestined to violence and death, ever be called free: free to choose and free to act or not act? It is my belief that this reservation is precisely the point.

II

Aristotle awarded the palm for classic tragedy to the *Oedipus Tyrannus* of Sophocles. If this is not quite the same thing as saying Oedipus is the most perfect example of the tragic protagonist, perhaps he will do for comparison. Everyone knows his tragic story, at least in outline, for it is one of the ironies of history that he has given his name to the folklore of psychology. In that same folklore, we in the modern world give tacit agreement to the belief that human free will is all but impossible. In the Greek world, once the oracle had spoken, who was ever so hopelessly "predestined" as Oedipus?

But, as everybody knows, that is not it at all. Oedipus becomes tragic only because he does strive against the prediction. Resolved to know, he goes to the oracle himself and hears the dire prophecy repeated. His mistake is in believing that by running away he can circumvent the dreadful events. His *hubris* lies in thinking he has escaped by his own strength and cleverness and in boasting that such is the case. But we know what he does not know, that far from escaping his destiny, he has run full tilt to meet it. When we first see him he is *tyrannus*, "first of men," a king who has made himself king by strength and cunning. But there is more dramatic irony: the tyrannos who killed the sphinx and assumed the throne and the queen is really the rightful ruler of Thebes, the true son of Laius. His confidence still unbroken, he is convinced he can save Thebes again as he did before. He pronounces the curse on the unknown polluter of the city, and as the process of ferreting out the guilty one goes on, Oedipus' search becomes one of finding his own identity. As the dark hints begin to accumulate, he boasts of his contempt for prophecy; his father is still alive and his mother is far away. As the flawlessly plotted action unfolds, there comes the crushing peripeteia: all along he had been nearer home than he knew.

We could say that Oedipus' fault lies in trying to beat the rap. But again, everyone knows that his tragedy has to mean more than that; that this expenditure of human striving and achievement and suffering has to stand for something grave and constant in the eternal human condition. It is very true that his is the classical *hubris*, the sin of pride and arrogance and over-confidence in his own ability. But far more to our purpose, we can say it is a failure to achieve self-knowledge, a failure of self-definition. Oedipus is saddled with an incredibly horrible, inevitable future. He has not asked for it and has done nothing to deserve it; it is all "decided" before he is born. But he persists and demands to know the truth. Bernard Knox has noted how in the Greek original there is the constant, cruelly ironic inter-running of *Oedipus, oidi* ("swell," as with pride or arrogance), and *oida*, "I know," a word that is often, too often, in Oedipus' mouth. At the beginning of the play there is too much that he does not know, and at the end there is too much that he does. It is in the interweaving of guilt and innocence, in the willing of his own actions, in the god-like insistence on knowing *who* he is and the crushing ruin that this knowledge brings him, that the tragic glory of Oedipus lies.

Consider another hero. About his birth there is mystery also. He too is spirited away as an infant because dreadful things are whispered about him, and he too is brought up by foster-parents whom he leaves hurriedly for fear he may have killed his foster-father. In a direct way, it can be said that his very begetting caused the death of his real father. He brings terrible shame, agony, and death to his real mother. After a great deal of wandering, he returns to that part of the world which, unknown to him, is the scene of his begetting and birth. Early in life he was given a free choice of two lines of conduct, one of which would have removed all danger from him. He persists in the other because it is necessary to the terms of his own definition of himself. He lives connubially with an older woman, who, as a result of his drive toward self-definition, dies a horrible death. The fearful rumors about him break out afresh. There is an old, mad visionary who claims to have special insight into the truth about him, and as a result, his fellow men are convinced he is a ritual pollution in the community. Pursued by them, he is harried for days and is eventually sacrificed in a particularly horrible ritual murder. He has been saddled with a terrible, inevitable curse. He did not ask for it and does nothing to deserve it; it was all "decided" before he was born. The second hero is, of course, Joe Christmas.

III

If the fall of Oedipus comes as a direct result of his terribly mistaken idea of who he is and his insistence on finding out, then the death of Joe Christmas is a result of his insistence that he already knows who he is and his persistence in the demand for the right to be himself, to live on the terms of his own self-definition. To state the paradox in another way, the classic tragic protagonist such as Oedipus, Othello, Hamlet, or Macbeth rejoices in an existence that allows him a superb scope of action in which to achieve self-realization, including self-knowledge, even though in this same drive toward self-fulfillment he destroys himself. The modern tragic protagonist, the hero of a Dostoyevsky, a Conrad, a Kafka, a Faulkner, a Hemingway, or a Warren, must use all his intelligence, his strength, his luck, merely to travel the tightrope between Cosmic Chaos on the one hand and Cosmic Absurdity on the other. He can trust in nothing, hope for nothing, and accept nothing at face value until he has put it to the test. He may have heard of determinism, but he does not believe in it; in the face of those joyous theories of self-exculpation formulated by present-day psychology and sociology that presumably give the individual the right to scream, "It's not my fault! It's not my fault!" his preference is much nearer the dreadful freedom of the existentialist: since existence is prior to essence, the individual is totally free and totally accountable for his own view of things, for with total freedom comes total responsibility.

In the case of Joe Christmas, Faulkner takes pains to make this freedom absolute. Here we must be blunt: previous critical opinion seemed almost never to be aware of that freedom. Partly because, one supposes, the term "conditioning" is now a household word, it was decided that Christmas is the helpless victim of his own conditioning. But surely it is obvious that the wellspring of all his actions is his refusal to surrender to that conditioning.

One of Faulkner's clearest strokes of genius is in leaving the question of whether Christmas has Negro blood unanswered. We, no one, will ever know if he has it or not. If he does have it, the percentage is very small, something that not only adds to the irony but leaves him free to "pass" if he chooses. Although he is, largely through the efforts of Old Doc Hines, putatively a Negro child at the orphanage, he is adopted and brought up as a white child by the McEacherns. ("He don't look no more like a nigger than I do," says a white character.) This is probably the most crucial point in the book. Christmas is free to choose what he will be, and his freedom is infinite. Precisely as Oedipus, he must find out who and what he is. One remembers a scene in the orphanage: Old Doc Hines is recalling how the five-year-old Christmas begins following the Negro yard-boy around:

> ... until at last the nigger said, 'What you watching me for, boy?' and he said, 'How come you are a nigger?' and the nigger said, 'Who told you I am a nigger, you little white trash bastard?' and he says, 'I ain't a nigger,' and the nigger says, 'You are worse than that. You dont know what you are. And more than that, you wont never know. You'll live and you'll die, and you wont never know. ...' [1]

But he must know, as with his determination to keep his own name. And because he is free, he cannot ever passively acquiesce. He cannot let others tell him how or what to be. All his life, people attempt to force him to be what they insist he must be: McEachern's beating him to inculcate worship of the Moloch-Jehovah; Mrs. McEachern's sickening attempts to make him as cringing as herself; Joanna Burden's final insistence that he "become a nigger." His method is active. In the fifteen years of wandering he tries life as a black man living with Negroes and as a white man attempting to live with whites. But ultimately he chooses to be neither—he will simply be himself. Until the very end, the community cannot decide what he is; their deep distrust grows from

---

[1] William Faulkner, *Light in August* (New York: Modern Library, 1950), p. 336.

his refusal to declare himself one or the other in a social pattern in which this is the most important distinction of all. He will insist on his right simply to be; he has defined himself and has fought hard for the definition. The murder of Joanna Burden and his own death are the fruits of that insistence.

Granted he has freedom and choice; what about rank and fortune? The modern hero, like Oedipus and Macbeth, makes his own. Christmas' distinction lies in the strength of his proud, ruthless, arrogant, cold self-sufficiency, as rigid as that of a Richard or an Ahab and more adequate to the strain placed upon it than Macbeth's. As with any modern hero, the simple fact that he is still alive may be as much good fortune as he can expect. It is far more important to prove he is typically human.

Part of the difficulty in understanding Christmas again lies in the form and structure of the novel. The sequence of telling is such that he is first seen as the utterly sinister alien and is revealed early in the book as a brutal murderer. It is only as the flashbacks begin to unfold and we see him as a child and youth that we are made aware of his simple humanity. He is presented for the most part at a distance, and his inmost thoughts and feelings are not often enough open to us. However, at rare intervals a momentary flash of insight will give a total revelation: for instance, we see the denial of love and belonging in the orphanage and the beatings by McEachern. The effect of these is of course cumulative, but the moment of revelation comes when Christmas hears his name will be changed:

> "He will eat my bread and he will observe my religion," the stranger said. "Why should he not bear my name?"
> The child was not listening. He was not bothered. He did not especially care, anymore than if the man had said the day was hot when it was not hot. He didn't even bother to say to himself *My name aint McEachern. My name is Christmas* There was no need to bother about that yet. There was plenty of time.[2]

We are shown the idyllic relationship with Bobbie, the stunted and no-longer-young waitress who is a working prostitute in her spare time. His slipping away from the McEachern farm at night to be with her is part of his program of defiance, but it is truly, at least at the beginning, the adolescent's first tentative, awestruck

---

[2] *Ibid.*, p. 127.

discovery of the body of the beloved and all its possibilities. Again, before the dawn of the day on which he will murder Joanna Burden, when the pressures that will compel either murder or complete surrender are building past endurance, he muses on the past:

> ... it seemed to him, sitting on the cot in the dark room, that he was hearing a myriad [of] sounds of no greater volume—voices, murmurs, whispers: of trees, darkness, earth; people: his own voice; other voices evocative of names and times and places—which he had been conscious of all his life without knowing it, which were his life, thinking *God perhaps and me not knowing that too* He could see it like a printed sentence, fullborn and already dead *God loves me too* like the faded and weathered letters on a last year's billboard *God loves me too.*[3]

His humanity, and perhaps even his own completely tragic awareness of his situation, is revealed in that incredible week in which we run with him while he eludes mobs, sheriff, deputies, Lucas, and bloodhounds. All that has gone before in the novel is brilliantly recapitulated as Christmas, still wrapped in the rags and tatters of his self-sufficiency and pride, works himself slowly away from the violence of the attack on the Negro church toward his tragic reconciliation with his fate, his acceptance of the price and the risk of the human condition. The incidents of his life which have "pre-destined" him toward the proud denial of his own humanity are echoed. Aware, as perhaps never before, of the simple joy of merely being alive and breathing, he watches another day begin:

> It is just dawn, daylight: that gray and lonely suspension filled with the peaceful and tentative waking of birds. The air, inbreathed, is like spring water. He breathes deep and slow, feeling with each breath himself diffuse in the neutral grayness, becoming one with loneliness and quiet that has never known fury or despair. 'That was all I wanted,' he thinks, in a quiet and slow amazement. 'That was all, for thirty years. That didn't seem to be a whole lot to ask in thirty years.'[4]

"That didn't seem to be a whole lot to ask. ..." No, it is not—simply the right to live and be one's own self, to expect perhaps a little peace, a little love; but knowing the price. (Who now hears

---

[3] *Ibid.,* p. 91
[4] *Ibid.,* p. 289.

the far-off echo of Thomas Jefferson: "We hold these truths to be self-evident . . . ?") But Christmas' dilemma is the truly tragic one: he is caught not between right and wrong but between right and right. Rejected, feared, hated, he has sought and been proud of that rejection and fear; but pushed too far he has gone too far, and unable to reconcile conflicting responsibility, he has committed a brutal murder.

Now he must go back. But it is impossible to go back, only forward. He must accept responsibility for the freedom of choice he exercised in his actions and pay the price of that freedom. But because he is truly tragic, he will not practice a mere passiveness and wait for the men with the dogs to come up and shoot him. He will actively seek his human reconciliation: his problem is how to begin to get back inside the human community. It is not easy; he has been isolated for too many years. He waits in the dawn for a farmhouse to come alive and the men to leave for the fields. Then he approaches the farm wife, who recognizes him, and quietly, from a respectful distance, he asks: "Can you tell me what day this is? I just want to know what day this is." [5]

Even though the white woman sends him away, the symbolism is clear. He wants to begin again by reaccepting the limitations of one of the most human and communal inventions: time. The next step involves a basic human need and social ritual. Having violently rejected the offer of food on a number of symbolic occasions, he approaches a Negro cabin to ask for a meal.

> He was sitting at a table, waiting, thinking of nothing in an emptiness, a silence filled with flight. Then there was food before him, appearing suddenly between long, limber black hands fleeing too in the act of setting down the dishes. It seemed to him that he could hear without hearing them wails of terror and distress quieter than sighs all about him, with the sound of the chewing and the swallowing. 'It was a cabin that time,' he thought. 'And they were afraid. Of their brother afraid.' [6]

He has made his first gestures, but it is not enough. He stops two Negro children and a Negro man to ask again the day of the week. They fear him as wildly as do the whites and reject him also. So, having shaved himself as carefully as he can with the razor, the murder weapon, he strikes across country to find his way to

---

[5] *Ibid.*, p. 290.
[6] *Ibid.*, pp. 292–93.

Mottstown. Given a ride on a wagon by a Negro youth who does not know who he is, he reviews his life:

> ... he is entering it again, the street which ran for thirty years. It had been a paved street, where going should be fast. It had made a circle and he is still inside of it. Though during the last seven days he has had no paved street, yet he has traveled farther than in all the thirty years before. And yet he is still inside the circle. 'And yet I have been farther in these seven days than in all the thirty years,' he thinks. 'But I have never got outside that circle. I have never broken out of the ring of what I have already done and cannot ever undo,' he thinks quietly, sitting on the seat, with planted on the dashboard before him the shoes, the black shoes smelling of Negro: that mark on his ankles the gauge definite and ineradicable of the black tide creeping up his legs, moving from his feet upward as death moves.[7]

The symbol is perfectly chosen. For thirty centuries or so, the black-white, light-dark, Apollonian-Dionysian, rational-irrational opposition has existed in Western civilization. If this were the only meaning of the symbol, its use would be forgivable but hardly brilliant. It should be remembered that Christmas gleefully exchanged his own shoes for these that had been worn by a Negro woman, to throw the bloodhounds off the scent. (At this stage, Christmas, like Oedipus, is "full of devices.") But now, completely alone, he is feared and rejected by both black and white. Urged on by the frantic greed of Lucas Burch and the fanatic madness of Old Doc Hines, the white community considers Christmas a Negro, hunts him as a Negro, and will lynch and mutilate him as a Negro. Continuing to wear the shoes, he looks at that mark "moving upward from his feet as death moves." The murder he committed was the direct result of his refusal to choose, black or white. While choice of action remains (which may not be long), he will *choose* his means of reconciliation. Had he chosen sooner, or had he merely gone away, as he was also free to do, Joanna Burden would not be dead, and he himself would not be about to die. As surely as he sees the blackness (his acceptance of Negro status) creep up his body, so surely his body is sinking into the darkness, the extinction, of death. He walks quietly about the streets of Mottstown until he is captured.

At this point only the last of the tragedy remains to be played

---

[7] *Ibid.*, pp. 296–97.

out. The reader may decide that Christmas has been unable to sustain his resolution, that his breaking away from the officers only to be shot and castrated by Percy Grimm reveals an artistic defect on the part of Faulkner. But Oedipus and Lear have moments toward the end when the old rage and arrogance blaze out. Antigone, St. Joan, Richard—all have moments when human fear of absolute extinction overwhelms human integrity. The moment is there for a conscious artistic purpose: to give us that ultimate awareness of pity and terror by reminding us that the protagonist is not a hollow tragic mask but a living human being, only a little less lucky than ourselves. There is a further meaning: free to the end, Christmas has held on to his life until this proper moment has come to give it, the moment most filled with reconciliation.

As Gavin Stevens says, no one will ever know what Christmas hoped for from Hightower, but it was the conflict in his blood that let him run but would not let him escape, that made him snatch up the pistol but would not let him kill Grimm with it. (It is Stevens who posits the black-white opposition. Faulkner has never said if there is Negro blood or not.) The meaning has taken on almost universal significance. It is the light-dark opposition that is in the blood of all of us; the savage pull between bright rationality and the darkness so feared by the Greeks, that leads to irrationality and death.

Little else in modern literature has the speed and inevitable onward sweep of the chapter in which Percy Grimm pursues Christmas and kills him. Taken merely as evocative realism, the writing is superb: the shots, the shouting; the blind rushes and clotted confusion of the mob; the added detail of the fire siren, a characteristic sound of our time, screaming the rise and fall of its meaningless message; the early resolution of the pursuit into a personal contest between Christmas and Grimm. The rendition of Grimm as a type is as merciless as anything else of the sort ever done. Grimm is as the embodiment of pure force so often is: his rather colorless personality and appearance are in ghastly disproportion to his ability to produce evil and violence. He is Faulkner's equivalent of the classic Nemesis of the Furies—machine-like, unerring, impersonal, mindless. Here the problem of belief is no problem at all.

Still guided perhaps by his irrational hope, Christmas runs into Hightower's house holding the pistol he has snatched up on the way. He could kill Grimm easily, but with nothing to lose by another killing, he does not; this is his final gesture of human reconciliation. Grimm empties the magazine of his automatic into Christmas' body, but this is not all.

> When the others reached the kitchen they saw the table flung aside now and Grimm stooping over the body. When they approached to see what he was about, they saw that the man was not dead yet, and when they saw what Grimm was doing one of the men gave a choked cry and stumbled back into the wall and began to vomit. Then Grimm too sprang back, flinging behind him the bloody butcher knife. "Now you'll let white women alone, even in hell," he said. But the man on the floor had not moved. He just lay there, with his eyes open and empty of everything save consciousness, and with something, a shadow, about his mouth. For a long moment he looked up at them with peaceful and unfathomable and unbearable eyes. Then his face, body, all, seemed to collapse, to fall in upon itself, and from out the slashed garments about his hips and loins the pent black blood seemed to rush like a released breath. It seemed to rush out of his pale body like the rush of sparks from a rising rocket; upon that black blast the man seemed to rise soaring into their memories forever and ever. They are not to lose it, in whatever peaceful valleys, beside whatever placid and reassuring streams of old age, in mirroring faces of whatever children they will contemplate old disasters and newer hopes. It will be there, musing, quiet, steadfast, not fading and not particularly threatful, but of itself alone serene, of itself alone triumphant. Again from the town, deadened a little by the walls, the scream of the siren mounted toward its unbelievable crescendo, passing out of the realm of hearing.[8]

They are not to lose it, nor, I think, are we. In Stephen Dedalus' terms, we feel pity and terror to a degree that is almost unbearable. One does not know why we feel these emotions or even less why the tragic spectacle is so compelling. It may be that it is better that we don't know. Certainly, as Nietzsche claimed, the tragic emotions lurk in the dark, irrational part of the blood, and very likely the rational mind wants no part of them. "Pity is the feeling which arrests the mind in the presence of whatsoever is grave and constant in human sufferings and unites it with the human sufferer." This part at least is no problem. We unite with Joe Christmas because he is the modern Everyman. In a cosmos where the only constants are absurdity and instability, we have the right to expect anything except rationality. Any one of us could become the victim. His suffering far transcends the time and place and means

---

[8] *Ibid.*, pp. 406–7.

Faulkner has used and comes to stand for everything that is grave and constant in the human condition.

"Terror is the feeling which arrests the mind in the presence of whatsoever is grave and constant in human suffering and unites it with the secret cause." The union with the secret cause is almost as terrible as the suffering itself, because it gives a moment of true insight into ourselves. Part of this insight is perfectly symbolized in *Light in August* when the injured Hightower, in a scene that might have come straight out of Dostoyevsky, is working himself toward complete self-knowledge. As the wheel of his memory turns on and on, he comes to realize that his own cold selfishness, his absorption in the Confederate grandfather, has caused his wife's disgrace and death. As the crowd of faces in his memory struggles to come into focus, one of them becomes the dead face of Christmas, but the focus is not clear; another face is struggling with that face, struggling to become clear and be recognized. Suddenly it emerges: it is the face of Percy Grimm, gunman, mutilator, avenging fury, lyncher extraordinary. Hightower never saw either of them before the lynching, but their terrible failure and terrible guilt are somehow directly related to his own failure to live up to his humanity. Somewhere at the root of the secret cause of things as they are, we are all related; we are all involved. We are all responsible because we are all a part of mankind. So far as the rational mind goes, the union with the secret cause is a moment of awareness, of realizing that grave and constant human suffering is truly constant. Once we achieve this awareness, the acceptance of the tragic human situation, with all its absurdity and irrationality, becomes possible, and with the acceptance come the emotions of peace and tranquility.

Yet the union with the secret cause has another side, which is less commendable. This emotion, which we are not so willing to let swim up to conscious awareness, can be curtly put as "There but for the Grace of God. . . ." The hero has fallen, but we, for the moment at least, are safe. Let society pick its victims as it pleases, so long as the victim is not I. It is in just this area of playing upon our deep, instinctual fears and misgivings that Faulkner has succeeded in achieving a favorable comparison with classic tragedy. It was impossible to put the Furies believably on the stage, but Faulkner found the perfect equivalent in the lynch mob, which one way or another elicits a strong emotion in all of us, or better still, a mixed one. In an age in which the very name of Oedipus has been explained away, tamed and embalmed in the clinic, in which almost no one can truly feel why Macbeth should think the murder of a king so much worse than any murder, and in which no one believes in the absurdity of an ancestral curse, the beholder is simply asked: "Did Joe Christmas inherit a curse?" Or rather, it is not necessary to ask, since we know. Faulkner has used the subconscious fear of mutilation and distrust of miscegenation that lurks in all of us, the love of and response to violence and death, the simultaneous love and hate of the loved one, to arouse these emotions or their equivalents in us. We love the violence and evil because we acquiesce in them. No doubt these emotions are despicable, but no doubt the emotions aroused by the spectacle of what Oedipus did were despicable also. The doctor who tamed the legend of Oedipus and rechristened it a complex only found out very late what the Christian world had known all along: when there are guilt and filth in the human psyche, the only possible remedy is to cast them out.

IV

This chapter has dealt only with the analysis of Joe Christmas as a modern tragic protagonist. It has hardly mentioned the many other excellences of *Light in August*, leaving until a later chapter the cases of Joanna Burden and Hightower, who are also classic examples of the tragedy of isolation, strongly underlining the case of Christmas.

Tradition tells us that the Greeks demanded that each trilogy submitted in the great dramatic contests be accompanied by an outrageous and lewd satyr play, which preferably would burlesque the very elements and events just presented as tragedy. Perhaps some such comic relief is essential. After the human emotions have endured all they can, after the *katharsis*, something has to sustain us until we can touch earth again. Perhaps this is one explanation of the bawdy, almost folksy humor of the Lena-Byron episode in the last chapter of *Light in August*, so often dismissed with bewilderment or anger as an artistic botch. The direct experience of pity and terror is a little like being caught up in a cyclone, or to use another metaphor, like being at the heart of what goes on in a thermonuclear explosion. In contemplating the question, "When will I be blown up?" the author of *Light in August* has always been willing to risk a small side bet on Mankind. This risk and this faith are also a part of the tragic paradox. The Greeks knew, as did the Elizabethans after them, that, in contemporary terms, once the mushroom cloud has blown away and the fallout has ceased to fall there is always the continuing residue of humanity. It, as the author would no doubt say, will endure.

B. R. McElderry, Jr.

Appendix:
The Narrative Structure
of *Light in August*

The Narrative Structure of Faulkner's *Light in August*

Day	Ch.	FORWARD ACTION / IMMEDIATE PAST / REMOTE PAST
Sat.	1	Lena's arrival in Jefferson. Burden fire sighted.
Sat.	2	Brown's association with Joe Christmas explained.
		Byron identifies Brown as Burch (Lena's seducer).
	3	Hightower's life in Jefferson. His wife's scandalous death. Loss of his church. His delivery of the Negro baby.
Sun.	4	Byron tells Hightower of Lena's search for Brown (Burch), of the fire, of the murder of Joanna Burden.
Fri.	5	Christmas quarrels with Brown, goes to town, returns: "Something is going to happen to me."
	6–7–8–9	Christmas at orphanage, adopted by McEacherns, meets waitress and tells her he is part Negro, beats up McEachern at dance, is himself beaten by waitress's friends.
	10	Christmas, three years before the murder, enters Joanna Burden's kitchen.
	11	Christmas seduces Joanna Burden.
		Story of the Burden family, abolitionists settled in the South.
	12	Christmas resents Joanna's increasing domination.
Fri.		Christmas murders Joanna when she draws a pistol.
Fri.		Christmas commandeers a car to further his escape.

From *College English*, XIX (February, 1958), 200–207. Reprinted by permission of the National Council of Teachers of English and of the author.

Sat.	13	Sheriff investigates murder.
Tues.		Byron tells Hightower he is moving Lena to Brown's cabin at Burden place.
Wed.		Hightower learns that Christmas's trail has been found.
Wed.		Hightower urges Byron to leave Lena.
Wed.	14	Deputy reports Lena staying at Brown's cabin.
Tues.		Christmas disturbs Negro church.
Fri. after murder		Christmas captured at Mottstown.
Fri.	15	Hineses learn of Christmas's capture.
Sun.	16	Through Byron, Mrs. Hines asks Hightower to give false alibi for her grandson, Christmas. Hightower refuses. Byron takes Hineses to Lena's cabin.
Mon.	17	Lena's baby born. Byron, previously refused by Lena, quits his job.
Mon.	18	Brown, taken by deputy to see Lena, escapes.
Mon.		Brown, pursued by Byron, beats him up.
Mon.		Byron learns Christmas has been killed.
Mon.	19	Lawyer Stevens puts Hineses on train, promising to send Christmas's body for burial.
Mon.		Christmas escapes, is shot and castrated by Percy Grimm.
	20	Hightower's early life—his Civil War father and grandfather, his invalid mother, his marriage to the minister's daughter.
Mon.		Hightower's death.*
	21	The traveling furniture dealer's story of Byron's doglike faithfulness to Lena, and her eventual acceptance of him.

Light in August:
The Two Actions Chronologically Arranged

The story of Lena and Byron is told in the following chapters: 1–2, meeting in Jefferson. 4, Byron's account of Lena, given to Hightower. 13, Byron moves Lena to Brown's cabin at the Burden

---

* In *Faulkner in the University* (Charlottesville: University of Virginia Press, 1959), p. 75, Faulkner explicitly says that Hightower did not die. [Editor's note]

place. 14, Deputy reports Lena living in Brown's cabin. 17, Lena's baby born. 18, Brown, confronting Lena, abandons her and later beats up Byron. 21, Byron accompanies Lena, and is eventually accepted by her.

The story of Joe Christmas is told in the following chapters: 15, Birth of Joe Christmas (told by the Hineses, his grandparents). 6–7–8–9–10, Joe's early life (orphanage, adoption by the McEacherns, affair with the waitress, fifteen years of wandering, meeting with Joanna Burden). 5, Events leading up to Joe's murder of Joanna. 12, Scene immediately before the murder. 1, First mention of the fire which broke out after the murder. 13, Sheriff's investigation of the murder. 4, Brown's story (as told to Hightower by Byron). 13–14, Christmas's trail to Mottstown. 15, Hines tried to incite, Mrs. Hines to prevent the lynching of Christmas. 16, Hightower refuses to give false alibi for Christmas. 19, Christmas killed when he escapes and takes refuge in Hightower's house. (According to Stevens, this was at the suggestion of Mrs. Hines.) Hightower does give the false alibi, but in vain.

The principal episodes from the remote past are as follows: 3, 17, 20, Hightower's early life. 11, Joanna Burden's family history and early life. 6–7–8–9–10, Joe Christmas's early life (listed above).